OPTIONS TRADING CRASH COURSE

THE BEGINNER'S GUIDE TO BECOME A SUCCESSFUL TRADER, STARTING OPTIONS, FOREX, DAY, AND SWING TRADING. WITH SIMPLE AND PROVEN STRATEGIES

BY JOHN SCOTT

© **Copyright 2019 - All rights reserved.**

The content contained within this book may not be reproduced, duplicated or transmitted without direct written permission from the author or the publisher.
Under no circumstances will any blame or legal responsibility be held against the publisher, or author, for any damages, reparation, or monetary loss due to the information contained within this book. Either directly or indirectly.

Legal Notice:

This book is copyright protected. This book is only for personal use. You cannot amend, distribute, sell, use, quote or paraphrase any part, or the content within this book, without the consent of the author or publisher.

Disclaimer Notice:

Please note the information contained within this document is for educational and entertainment purposes only. All effort has been executed to present accurate, up to date, and reliable, complete information. No warranties of any kind are declared or implied. Readers acknowledge that the author is not engaging in the rendering of legal, financial, medical or professional advice. The content within this book has been derived from various sources. Please consult a licensed professional before attempting any techniques outlined in this book.

By reading this document, the reader agrees that under no circumstances is the author responsible for any losses, direct or indirect, which are incurred as a result of the use of information contained within this document, including, but not limited to, — errors, omissions, or inaccuracies.

Table of Contents

INTRODUCTION: 6
CHAPTER 1: AN OVERVIEW OF OPTION 9
CHAPTER 2: WHAT ARE OPTIONS 14
CHAPTER 3: OPTION TERMINOLOGY 19
CHAPTER 4: EXERCISING THE OPTION 23
CHAPTER 5: DESIGNING A TRADING PLAN: 28
CHAPTER 6: TRADING PSYCHOLOGY 33
CHAPTER 7: RISK MANAGEMENT, ... 39
CHAPTER 8: TRADING AS A BUSINESS 44
CHAPTER 9: TECHNICAL ANALYSIS. 49
CHAPTER 10: SEARCHING FOR TRADE. 55
CHAPTER 11: DAY TRADING RULES. 60
CHAPTER 12: OPTION STRATEGIES. 65
CHAPTER 13: WHAT IS FOREX 70
CHAPTER 14: DAY TRADING 75
CHAPTER 15: SWING TRADING AND STRATEGIES. 81
CHAPTER 16: CALLS AND PUTS 86
CHAPTER 17: OPTIONS TRADING AND THE INDIVIDUAL INVESTOR 90
CHAPTER 18: CANDLESTICK CHARTS AND PATTERNS 95
CHAPTER 19: GENERAL POSSIBILITIES OF SOLVING BEGINNERS ERRORS .. 100
CHAPTER 20: OPTIONS GREEKS 105
CHAPTER 21: THE BEST FIVE OPTION TRADING STRATEGIES 109
CHAPTER 22: DO'S AND DON'TS 113
CHAPTER 23: BUYING AND SELLING PUTS 118
CHAPTER 24: THE MOST COMMON QUESTIONS ABOUT TRADING 123
CONCLUSION: 126

Introduction

Options trading might seem like a new concept, but it's been around for a long time. It is believed that the first person ever to trade options was a man named Thales. Back in 332 BC, Thales made a fortune by buying the rights to purchase olive before harvest. How did he do that? Let's see.

The first instance of options trading 332 BC

Aristotle writes about Thales in his book Politics, which he wrote in 332 BC. It sounds incredible that humans would have used the concept of options - trading the rights to assets without purchasing the assets themselves - so far back in the past, but it is indeed true.

Thales was a smart man. What he did was observe the patterns of the weather and the stars, and then predicted a big olive harvest soon. A brilliant plan formed in his mind. He decided to use a small amount of money to secure the rights to all olive presses in the area. So, you can say that this was a call option with the underlying assets being olive presses. His prediction turned out to be correct, and the harvest was bountiful. He then proceeded to sell his rights to those who needed them and made a considerable fortune for himself in the process.

But there's another side to this story. The respective owners of the olive presses in the area were perhaps the first humans to ever use a Covered Call strategy, meaning that they turned out profits by selling the options to Thales, regardless of how the product turned out to be. This was the procedure that would define how options trading would function for centuries to come.

Options trading in London through the 18th century

The first instance of both call and put options appearing in the organized market together was around the late seventeenth century in London, after the tulip mania of 1636 when tulip prices were widely speculated upon. Options are inherently speculative, so the trade volume was really low. Opposition towards options trading was continually growing, and eventually, it became illegal to trade options in London. Ignorance and fear are compelling reasons, after all. Options trading remained illegal in London for more than a hundred years, from 1733 to 1860.

The onset of options trading in the US circa 1872

The first person to create a call and put options in the US was Russell Sage in 1872. Born in New York, he was a famous American Financier. He started to make a career for himself in politics but pivoted into finance in 1874 when he bought a seat in the New York Stock Exchange. When he died in 1906, he had a vast fortune of $70 million. He created the first Over-the-counter options in the US, and even though they were far from liquid and quite unstandardized, they still made him a ton of fortune in just a few years.

Sage lost a lot of his fortune, however, in the market crash of 1884, and this led to him giving up options entirely. Nevertheless, the OTC options market that he had set up no longer required his participation to continue functioning and growing. The market was unregulated until SEC was established after the great depression.

The establishment of CBOE and OCC in 1973

In the modern history of options trading, the most important event by far would be the formation of the Options Clearing Corporation (OCC) and the Chicago Board of Exchange (CBOE) in 1973. This is a milestone that has defined how public exchange options trading is done today.

As we already know, before the formation of CBOE, options were highly illiquid, unstandardized, and inefficient, given the fact that they were traded over the counter. CBOE regulated the options trading market by standardizing all the call options contracts and their terms. In 1973, the general public was able to trade call options for the first time with guaranteed performance and liquidity. Today, we continue to use this system.

They did the same for put options in 1977, and the options trading market as we know now was created. As the years have passed, more and more exchanges have been set up for trading, and much better computational models have been introduced.

Chapter 1: An Overview of Option

The majority of people have the notion that trading is a brand-new form of investment when compared to other forms of investment of the traditional style, for instance, buying stocks and shares. But, the modern face of options trading as we all know today was introduced a long ago during the formation of the CBOE, also known as the Chicago Board of Option Exchange. The modern-day options trading was introduced during the formation of CBOE but the basics of the same date back to the ancient times of Greece, as long as the 4th century BC. From that time only, options marked its presence in the market in several formats, and it was refined in the year 1973 after the foundation of CBOE. In that year only, options' trading was standardized correctly, and it gained immense credibility as well as popularity.

Olive Harvest

The earliest existence of options that has been recorded was found in a book that was composed during the 4th century BC by the famous philosopher from Greece, Aristotle. Aristotle wrote several books, and all of his works are also of significant influence. In the book 'Politics' written by him, Aristotle mentioned his encounter with another famous philosopher, Thales. How Thales was able to make a massive profit by harvesting olives has been mentioned in the book. Thales had a great interest in astrology along with mathematics. So, he came up with the very first recorded concept of options trading by combining all the knowledge that he acquired from various subjects of his interest. By studying the stars, Thales could predict that there was going to be a considerable olive harvest in his region. So, he was started decking up for profiting from his predictions. He was also able to analyze that there was going to be a rise in the overall demands of olive presses. So, his target was to corner the entire olive market.

But, despite all his planning, he faced the problem of not having enough funds to own the presses of olive. So, the next thing that he did was to pay all those individuals who owned their olive presses with a fixed sum of money so that he could secure all his rights to use them up at the correct time. As the harvesting time came by, the harvest was huge, as he already predicted before. He resold all the rights that be bought earlier to those people who were in need now. He made a huge profit by reselling all his rights. No form of terms was indeed used by Thales at that time but be created the first call option where he used the olive press rights as the underlying security.

Thales paid out for all his rights, but he didn't pay for any kind of obligation for the usage of the presses at a fixed price. He was also capable of exercising all the options to make a considerable amount of profit. This is the general principle that works out for call options today. The only difference that can be found today is that we now have various added factors in the whole setup, for example, financial instruments and commodities instead of the rights of olive presses for having them as the security.

The Tulip Bulb Mania of 17th Century

There was another occurrence in the ancient days that is relevant to the concept of options trading. It was an event that took place in the 17th century. The event occurred in Holland as it is called the Tulip Bulb Mania. In that period, there was great popularity and demand for tulips in that region. Tulips were even considered as a status symbol among the Dutch aristocrats. It became so popular in Holland that it spread all around the world, including Europe. This resulted in high demand for the tulip bulbs that used to increase in percentage with moving time at a high rate. By this time, calls and puts were already introduced in the market of trading, mainly because of hedging.

For example, the tulip bulb growers opted for buying options of put for protecting all their profits, if the price of the tulip bulbs reduced drastically. The tulip wholesalers opted for buying call options to protect themselves if the price of the bulbs increased drastically. It is worth taking into account that the contracts that were used in ancient times were not at all developed as they are today, and the market of the same was informal. It was not regulated as well.

During the early 1630s, the overall demand for the tulip bulbs increased drastically, and it was accompanied by an increase in the price of the bulbs than the standard value. Thus, the price of options contracts related to the price of the bulbs increased. There was also a development of a secondary market that was related to the options contracts that permitted all those individuals to speculate on the tulip market. As a result, many people started investing in all those contracts with huge sums, mostly by investing all their saved money or by borrowing money against some significant assets, such as property. The tulip bulb price kept on moving up but it could only rise until the tulip bulbs started to burst eventually.

The cost of tulip bulbs rose to a particular time that was entirely unsustainable at that time. This resulted in the vanishing of the buyers as the price of the tulip bulbs dropped down suddenly. All those individuals who opted to give in their all-in order to buy contracts were now wiped out. The economy of the Dutch entered a period of heavy recession. Only because the options market was not at all regulated; there was no other way in which the investors could be forced to fulfill all the related obligations of the options. Thus, options ended up earning a bad reputation worldwide.

Trading of Options and the Related Bans

Although options trading gained a bad name all over the world, there were still a huge number of investors who wanted to invest in the same. The main reason behind this was that the options contracts provided a great amount of power related to leverage, and that is the reason why they are so popular in the whole world today. Thus, it can be stated that contracts trading went along at its very own pace. Despite all these, the bad reputation acquired by options was pretty hard to be cleared. Also, an alarming opposition rose to the trading of the options. Checking back the history of options trading, it faced several bans throughout the world. It faced bans in Europe, Japan, and in various states of the USA.

One of the most notable bans was held by London. Even after the development of a greatly organized market for calls and puts in the late 16th century, the wall of opposition against options was still hard to break. This resulted in options being treated as an illegal activity during the 18th century. The ban that was imposed on options trading during the 18th century lasted for more than 100 years. The ban was not lifted until the mid-19th century.

Russell Sage

One of the greatest developments that were ever made in the course history of trading of options was the one that involved the association of an America-based financer, Russell Sage. In the late 19th century, Russell started creating options of calls and puts that came with the capability of being traded in the US over the counter. There was no presence of a formal market till that time, but Russell decided of creating a sort of activity that is taken as a breakthrough in the course of options trading. Also, Russell was the first person who built up a connection between options price, underlying security price, and interest rate. He even used up the principle of put-call parity for devising a synthetic form of loans.

This permitted Russell Sage to provide all other people with the amount of loan money at a fixed rate of interest. He could fix the rate after setting up the price of the contract, along with the individual strike price. But he stopped trading in his way right after he incurred some large amount of losses. But, despite the losses, Russell was the only instrument who became a part of the continuous evolution of options trading market. In the late 18th century, the brokers and dealers started placing advertisements to attract buyers and sellers of contracts with the target of deal brokering. The main goal behind this was that the customers who were interested would search for a proper broker for expressing their wish for either purchasing calls or puts on some definite stock. Right after that, the concerned broker would find someone for placing any part of the whole transaction. This was taken to be a tiring process.

The contract terms were properly determined by the related parties. The broker of calls and puts along with the Dealers Association wanted to develop a network that could provide them with the required help for matching the sellers with the buyers and vice versa in an easy way. But, even after that, there was no sign of standard pricing, and also the options market lacked in liquidity.

By this time, the options trading market was developing constantly, even though there was a lack of regulations that ultimately left all the investors in a state of wary.

Listed Options Market

The options trading market was still regulated largely by the put and call broker with the options contracts only being traded as over the counter. There was some form of standardization in the market that was visible. This resulted in a greater number of people to know about options trading and also their proper usage. But the market was still illiquid with only one form of activity at that time. The brokers were profiting heavily from the huge spread that was being paid by the buyers and what was being accepted by the sellers. But a proper pricing structure was still not available. So, the spread was effectively set up by the brokers, and they could regulate the same according to their needs.

Some regulations were standardized by the US Securities and Exchange Commission for the options trading market, but the trading rate was still not progressing, and that could be seen by the late 1960s. Several complexities got involved in the entire process, and it was turned into a really tough thing for the investors' whole considering any kind of option as the instrument of trading only because of the inconsistent price. In 1968, a considerable decline came into notice by the Chicago trade board in commodities trading. It started to search out for brand new ways by which it was possible to develop the business. The main aim was to create and diversify some added opportunities for each member of the exchange. After reviewing several alternatives, a final decision was made for creating an exchange of formal nature for all the contracts of trading that were linked to options.

Chapter 2: What are options

An option is a financial contract called a derivative contract. It allows the owner of the contract to have the right to buy or sell the securities based on an agreed-upon price by a specified period.

That definition is rather complicated so I will break it down into its components and explain each.

As the name suggests, there is no obligation in this type of transaction. The trader pays for the right or the option to buy or sell a transaction such as a security, stock, index or ETF (exchange-traded fund) by a certain amount of time. An option is a contract.

Derivative Contract

The option derives its value based on the value of the underlying asset hence the term derivative contract. This contract states that the buyer agrees to purchase a specified asset within a certain amount of time at a previously agreed-upon price. Derivative contracts are often used for commodities like gold, oil, and currencies, which is often in the form of the US dollars. Another type of derivative is based on the value of stocks and bonds. They can also be based on interest rates such as the yield on a specified amount of time Treasury note, like a 10-year Treasury note.

In a derivative contract, the seller does not have to own the specified asset. All he or she has to do is have enough money to cover the price of the asset to fulfill the contract. The seller also has the option of giving the buyer another derivative contract to offset the asset's value. These choices are often practiced because they are easier than providing the asset itself.

Securities

Securities come in several types. The great thing about securities is that they allow a person to own a specified asset without actually taking tenure of it. This makes them readily tradable because they are good indicators of the underlying value of the asset.

Common types of options securities include:

- Stock options, which use stock in a publicly listed company as the asset associated with the contract.

- Index options. Similar to stocks, an index is a measure of the stocks, bonds and other securities a company possesses.
- Currency options. Also referred to as forex options, this type of security grants the right to buy or sell a specific currency at a previously agreed-to exchange rate.
- Futures options, which gives the trader the right to assume a certain position at a future date.
- Commodity options, which is an option with an associated asset that is a physical commodity.
- Basket options. As the name suggests, this is an option made up of a group of securities.

Agreed-Upon Price

This is also known as the strike price. It does not change no matter how much time has passed and it is so named because the trader strikes when the underlying value makes him or her the desired income.

Specified Period

This is also known as the expiration date because this is the date at which the option (contract) expires. The trader can exercise the option at the strike price at any time up until the expiry date reaches. In some parts of the world such as Europe, a trader can only exercise the right to the option at the strike price exactly on the expiry date. We will more largely focus on the American way of trading options, which allows for exercising right on or before the expiration date.

Options vs. Stocks

Trading options and trading stocks are different because stocks and options have different characteristics. Stocks represent shares of ownership in individual companies or options. This allows the stock trader to bet in any direction that he or she feels the stock price is headed.

Stocks are a great investment if you are thinking of long-term yield such as for retirement and have the capital. They are very simplistic in the approach in that the trader buys the stock and wagers on the price that he or she thinks it will rise at a certain time in the future. The hope is that the price will increase in value, thus gaining the trader a substantial yield.

Stocks are also a great option for those who want to invest without having to keep a steady eye on the growth of the investment.

The risk of investing in stocks is that the price of stocks can plummet to zero at any moment. This means that the investor can lose his or her entire investment at the drop of a hat because stocks are very volatile from day to day. They are very reactive to world events such as wars, politics, scandal, epidemics and natural disasters.

On the other hand, options are a great option for traders who would like flexibility with timing and risks. The trader is under no obligation and can see how the trade plays out over the time specified by the option contract. In that time period, the price is locked which is also a great appeal.

Trading options also requires a lower investment compared to stocks typically.

Another great appeal for options reading is that the specified time period is typically shorter than investing in stocks. This allows for regular buying and selling as options have different expiration dates. Expiration dates can range from just a few days to several years.

The drawback that makes some people hesitate in trading options is that it is more complex than trading stocks. The trader needs to learn new jargon and vocabulary such as strike prices, calls and puts so that he can make the determination on how he or she can set up effective options. Not only does the trader have to learn new terms, but he or she also has to develop new skillsets and the right mindset for options trading.

Call Option

This type of option gives the trader the right to buy the asset on or before the expiration date. Also simply labelled a call, this type of option is traded because the price of the underlying asset is expected to rise within a certain timeframe. For the buyer of a call option, the profit lies in the price moving above the strike price. The trader can then sell the option to make a profit, which is the common call for most buyers or, choose the right to exercise the option on or before the expiration date.

The person who sells this type of option receives the premium from the trader to generate income. Therefore, the seller has a limited income while the buyer of such an option has an unlimited potential for profit.

Stocks are a common asset in call option transactions. An example of a successful call options transaction is specified below using stocks as the asset.

There are 100 shares of stock up for sale. Each share is priced at $100 and therefore, a stock trader would pay $10,000 to buy these.
As an options trader, you can buy a call option that will give you the right to pay this $100 per share within a specified time period of six months. The option would cost $5 per share and so, the options trader would pay a total of $500. This is a substantially lower investment than outright buying the stock. The risk is also lower than buying the stock as there is always the risk that the stock does not increase in value.

The trader had a good feeling that these stocks would increase in value though and they do by the expiration date. They are now worth $150 per share.

If the trader had bought the stock outright, he or she would make a profit of $5,000 because the stocks are now worth $15,000. As a call option, the trader would make a profit following the following formula:

(Current Price of the Stock - Strike Price) X Number of Shares = Option Worth

Using our example, this translated into:

($15,000 - $10000) x 100 = $5000

Next, to determine the profit the options trader would make, you need to remove the cost of the option. In this example, this cost was $500 and thus, the options trader makes a profit of $4,500. While this profit is slightly lower than what the stock trader made, the investment and risk were also substantially lower than outright buying the stock.

The general terms that show whether the options trader made a profit are:

- In the money. This means the asset price is above the call strike price as so the options trader makes a profit on the transaction.
- Out of the money. This means the price is below the call strike price and so the options trader makes a loss on the transaction.
- At the money. This means the asset price and the strike price are the same and so the options trader does not make a profit but neither does he or she make a loss on the transaction.

Put Option

This type of option gives the trader the right to sell the specified asset at the predetermined price by the expiration date. The strike price is also predetermined with this type of option. With a call option, the trader hopes that the price of the asset increases. However, with the put option, the trader hopes that the price of the asset goes down. Only if the price of the asset goes down does the trader make a profit.

Here is how this works... The trader pays for the option to sell the asset by a fixed time. If the price of the assets goes up, the trader has to sell the assets at a higher price if he or she exercises the right to the option. This is clearly a bad deal because the gap between the strike price and the selling price has narrowed.

On the other hand, exercising the right to sell the asset when it has depreciated in value widens the gap between the strike price and the sale price.

Let us take a look at how this works with an example using stock.

The trader has a feeling that 100 shares of stock will declining value in the near future. These 100 shares of stock are worth $100 per share now ($10,000 total). The put options trader purchase the right to sell the stock at any time within the next six months. The option costs $1.50 per share and so, the options trader pays $150.

Assuming that the options trader's gut feeling pays off and the value of the stock goes down to $50 per share by the time that the expiration date arrives, this is highly profitable. Exercising the right of the put option, the trader can sell the stock for the strike price of $100. The profit is calculated with this formula:

   Asset Value - Option Cost = Profit

Therefore, using our example the profit that the trader would earn:

   $10,000 - $150 = $9,850.

This is a much higher value than the $5,000 that would have been earned if the trader did not exercise the put option.

Chapter 3: Option terminology

Strike Price

For a call option, there is a fixed price that is a part of the contract, which allows the buyer to purchase any amount of stock corresponding to a specific company at a pre-determined. The set price contained in the contract can be termed as the "strike price". The strike price of this kind of contract is one of its most important characteristics, and when you go to look for options to trade, you are going to see them listed in order by strike price. So, who do you purchase the shares from? You would buy the shares from the seller of the options contract. In the event they were not able to fulfill their end of the deal, the broker would step in and do it for them (with consequences to the seller). The strike price must be used independently of the stock's current market valuation. As such, if there is a strike price of $50, but the stock's current market valuation has risen to $350 per share, it's not relevant. The seller of the call option would still be required by law to sell you 100 shares at $50 a share.

The concept is the same for put options. In this case, the strike price of this kind of contract entitles the holder to trade a specific amount of a stock. As in the case of call options, you would be selling the shares to the originator of the put option. They would be legally bound to buy the shares of the stock whose valuation has been determined by the seller regardless of its perceived current market valuation.

Expiration Date

Next, we come to the other crucial piece of information, which is the date of the expiration date of the contract itself. Generally speaking, the most common way in which options can be traded are listed is first by expiration date. When you select a given expiration date, you will then see options listed by strike price. On some platforms, options are all listed on the same page but grouped according to type. So, you will see all the call options listed at the top, and then this will be followed by the put options. In other cases, you will see a tab that lets you move back and forth between call and put options for the same expiration date.

As we will see, the expiration date is very important for many reasons. As this critical deadline approaches, if the contract does not have an appropriate valuation with regard to stock's current market valuation, it's going to be rapidly losing value. Let's get some insight into this with this sample situation. Let's assume that you are looking to purchase a contract for a call option that has a current strike valuation of $10. With this trade, you are looking to make a profit when its price increases. As such, the option has the greatest value when its current market valuation exceeds $10. Consequently, you profit more, the higher the price gets. Now, let's assume that its current market valuation falls to $7 instead. Then that call option simply isn't worth anything. People can just buy shares for $7, so why would anyone enter into a contract that required them to buy shares at $10 a share? Of course, they wouldn't do that. The longer you have remaining on the deal, the greater the value it has. If there are three months left on the contract, then it might still have a little value, because there would be a chance that the stock could move significantly in that time frame. But, if there are only three days left on the contract, the chances of the stock increasing from $7 to above $10 are pretty much nil (unless an earnings call is coming up and it turns out to be unexpectedly rosy), so the option will be rapidly losing value.

The expiration date is also important because when an option expires, it may be in a position where it can be exercised. Of course, there are as many approaches to this situation as there are unique individuals. Some people are small traders and simply don't want to buy or sell stock, and they may not have the capital to do so even if they wanted to. Remember, we are talking about 100 shares for each options contract.

On the other hand, others may be looking to buy and sell the shares. So, they may want to exercise the option when it expires, or even beforehand. If you are not able to buy and sell shares, you'll probably want to get out of the option before it expires to avoid this situation. In other words, you'll want to get whatever profits you can from selling the option. So, you want to sell it prior to the expiration date.

The expiration date is closely associated with a concept called time decay (and time value), so let's go ahead and discuss that.

Time Decay

Time decay is an important factor to consider when trading options. For buyers, time decay works against them. For options sellers (that is people who sell to open options contracts), time decay works in their favor.

Earlier, we touched on the basic idea of time decay. When there is a long time until the option expires, there is a higher probability that the price of the option can move in one direction or the other. That means that the market price of the shares can move in such a way as to make the option profitable. On the other hand, as time passes, that probability that this is going to happen decreases. In fact, each day, that probability drops. This is known as time decay.

Time decay actually refers to a drop in the price of the option on the options market. Options pricing is complicated and described by mathematical formulas, and a part of that is value that comes from the time remaining until the option expires. This value is called time value, and time value translates into real dollars and cents. Again, as we will see, there are several elements that influence the valuation of an options contract, so it might so happen that an option is gaining overall value even as it loses time value. Down below, we'll discuss that a little bit more. In other cases, time value will be dropping rapidly, and the price of the option is going to be dropping with it.

Time value is also known as extrinsic value. Time value is extrinsic because it only relates to the time remaining on the options contract. We are simplifying a little bit, but this is generally the way to think of it. So, it's not derived from the underlying market valuation for this stock. Pricing of the option that comes from the underlying stock is known as intrinsic value.

Options Chain

The list in which options for stocks and even index funds that are up for sale is known as the options chain. Every option has a ticker, although many modern platforms don't bother with that anymore since options information can be displayed in a user-friendly manner using computer and mobile technology. The options ticker includes information on the option such as which underlying stock the option is for, the expiration date, type of option, and the strike price. It might look something like this:

The first part of the options ticker is the stock ticker of the underlying stock or index fund for the option. This is followed by the expiration date, which is given in a 2-digit year, month, and day format.

This means January 3, 2020. So, the format is YYMMDD. Following this, we see a single letter representing the type of option. In the case of AMZN200103C1530000, since we see a C in this position, that means that we are dealing with a call option. Had it been a put option, we'd see AMZN200103P1530000.

The last part pertaining to the contract is its strike price. This valuation (strike price) will have three decimal places and leading zeros if the strike price uses up all the digits. In other words, 1530000 represents a strike price of $1,530. If the strike price had been $851, the ticker would look like this:

Tickers are displayed grouped by expiration date, with calls first, followed by put options, but probably with the ability to switch between them.

As we said, many platforms no longer use the tickers and simply display the options by strike price in a user-friendly, readable format. Below, we see the contrast between the traditional display used by Yahoo Finance, and a newer user-friendly display used by the mobile trading platform Robin Hood:

Here we see that you can simply click on a date at the top of the screen. For that date, we are able to move between call and put options with a single tap, and also between the purchase and sale. The options are listed in rows, going from highest strike price to lowest one, with the prevailing market valuation noted on the screen. The actual price of this contract is displayed on the right side of the screen, along with some other information.

How Options Are Priced

Options prices are quoted on a per-share basis. For the vast majority of options contracts, there are 100 underlying shares of stock. So, the quoted price is for one share, but to buy a single options contract, you'll be doing it for all 100 shares. Fractional purchases of options are not allowed. So, if you see the price of an option quoted as $2, that means to buy the option, you actually have to pay $200.

As you can see, some options are quite expensive, but the price varies considerably. In the example using Google above, the last option at the bottom has a price of $15.70. That means actually to buy this option. You must pay $1,570. Of course, looking at it another way, you could sell the option for $1,570, and that might clue you in as to why people are interested in selling options contracts. More on that later. Next, we are going to cover some industry jargon that refers to the relationship between the market valuation of the individual stock and its strike price.

In the Money

An option can be said to be *in the money* when it would be prudent to exercise it. In doing so, the transaction would generate a profit. As such, the term "in the money" means that the current valuation of a call options contract is greater than the current market price of the shares. The same can be said about a put options contract when its share price is below the valuation of the contract itself. But in reality, we need to take into account the price paid for the option. So, let's look at a more formal and more accurate definition.

Chapter 4: exercising the option

Practicing options are used when you need to change over your options spot into stock. Most option brokers never really need to change over their options to stock; in this manner, practicing options are seldom used.

There are times you might need to claim stock by changing over your options. To practice your options, you must make a long put or long a call.

Short options never can practice their options; short options must be allotted.

To return to our options, a long put gives you the privilege to sell the stock, and a long call gives you the privilege to buy a stock.

You now are long 1 contract of a TOP 40 call, and TOP is trading for $45. You concluded that you need to claim the TOP stock, so you practice the agreement. When you practice the agreement, you will buy 100 portions of TOP at $40 (the strike cost).

Presently, when you buy the stock, fight the temptation to go back and sell it for $45. If you plan just to buy the stock and pivot and trade them for a benefit, you would prefer not to work out. You can accomplish similar outcomes with less expense if you offer to close your position.

When we look at practicing a long put, you will sell the offers as opposed to buying the offers.

You are long 1 contract of a TOP 30 put, and TOP is trading at $25. You choose to short the stock, so you practice your agreement. When you practice the contract, you will short 100 portions of TOP at $30 (the strike cost).

Much the same as with our long call, you would prefer not to practice the agreement so you can quickly close the position and gather the profit. If that were the situation, you would offer to close your long put. This will enable you to get the profit at a lower expense.

If you need to practice your option, you should contact the option company and let them know about your expectations. A few financiers will have catches to assign that you need to practice your option. However, most businesses will have you bring in to affirm your arrangements. Most financiers are going to charge you an additional expense to practice your options. You can rapidly observe and think about your financier expenses at StockBrokers.com.

If your options are one-penny in-the-money at lapse, it will consequently be practiced by your business. Assuming that you want to practice your options, you have to finish it off with a buy to close or offer to close requests before termination. Holding up too long could be hindering to your portfolio. You could rest on Friday with 5 entries that are marginally in-the-money and wake up Monday with 500 portions of stock in your portfolio.

Don't Exercise/Practice out of the Money Options

Never practice an option which is out-of-the-money. Practicing options are intended for in-the-money options as they were. This is effectively clarified with a model.

You now are long a call at 50 strike. Your fundamental is at present trading at $40, and you choose to practice. Presently you have changed over your options into offers at $50.00 even though the basic is just trading at $40; you have a loss. If you needed to get the portions of the stock, you ought to have offered to close, finished off your options and bought the offers in the market for $40 rather than $50. Try not to set yourself up by beginning with a loss, just options that are exercise in-the-money.

Don't Exercise an Option Before Expiration

When practicing your options before termination, you are giving up the properties of the options for which you've officially paid.

In the first place, you will relinquish the time price of the options. If your basic is trading at $50, and you're on a long call options at the $45 strike, you will have at any rate a $5 benefit (50 - 45). If you practice your options before the expiry, that is your lone benefit on that position.

If you have time staying before the lapse, your call will have a greater benefit without anyone else's input. The benefit of your call would be $5 + time value. When you practice, you lose the time value.

You could offer to close the options in the market for more than $5 if it is before lapse. The closer you get to lapse, the more your time worth abatements until it comes to $0. Your call would be worth $5 at termination, and that is the point at which you practice.

You are long an approach the $30 strike that cost $3.00 and terminates in about fourteen days, and your fundamental is trading for $40. You concluded you're close enough to lapse and need to practice your call. You never again have those options and now hold 100 offers at $30. The following day an unexpected declaration is discharged that the organization is under scrutiny for misrepresentation. The stock starts to sink, and toward the day's end is worth $20. You are presently sitting on a $1,000 loss. If you had held those options, it would be useless now. However, your all-out loss would have just been $300.

Even though you will begin your options instruction finding out about practicing options at the strike value, you will find that you once in a while will practice genuine positions. Most options brokers never need to claim the stock. They trade options to deal with the agreements forward and backward.

When you buy to open, go long, or pay a net charge for a position, go long or open; you will use an offer to near close the position.

If you offer to open, go short, or get a net acknowledgment for a position, you will use a buy to near close the position.

Options aren't as risky as Wall Street would make it look. Infect, they can really limit risk. Here is an options trading strategy that can enable you to get huge twofold digit gains and overcome any potential losses.

Two rules or guidelines to follow every time you want to make a trade are:
1. Practice before spending real money on live trades.
2. For any trade, risk no more than 2% of your wallet.

Once in a while, however, you may detect a deal that you have faith in your heart can profit.

The main issue is it costs more than $500.

So, would you be able to, in any case, make a profit without totally overlooking risk management? The appropriate response is yes! Here's the ticket: Use put or call debit spread to hedge risk on a highly-priced option

Remember that your profit potential is boundless when buying calls, however your most extreme benefit potential when buying puts is constrained since the stock can just drop as low as zero. The most you stand to risk (or loss) on a long call is the measure of money you spent to gain entry to the trade. As said before, you only get to lose the money you spent on the trade, which is the only risk involved.

In a debit put or debit call spread, what you're doing is "selling to-open," an option opposite the one "bought to-open," which supports the danger of your trade. This implies you're at the same time selling and buying either puts or calls (on a similar request ticket) to counterbalance the expense of puts or calls bought.

Asides those, diagonal spreads are a magnificent long-haul approach to both contribute with options and produce some month to month income simultaneously. Numerous merchants really don't think a lot about how ground-breaking and adaptable these spreads can be for fruitful trading.

Diagonal option spreads are built up by getting into both a short and long position in two options of an identical sort (either two put or two call options) yet with various strike costs and termination dates.

Take one moment to process that and read it again, assuming that you have to. Basically, the technique is like a covered call, then again, actually, a long call is replaced with the stock.

This technique is called "diagonal" since it joins a level spread, which speaks to contrasts in lapse dates, with a vertical spread, which speaks to contrasts in strike costs. You could even consider it the posterity of vertical and calendar spread.

How and When to use a Diagonal Spread

One of the essential reasons you might close a diagonal spread is if you want to procure enough premium from the subsequent barter. Then again, you might be provoked to closing the trade should the close month option seem to go into-the-money, and you need to keep away from the capability of getting relegated on the sold options.

The following are a couple of investments to pursue when hoping to close a diagonal spread;

Get into a buy to-close request for the close termination contract that you had recently sold.

As a standard guideline, it is significant for you to, in every case in a diagonal spread, close the short side first for edge prerequisite reasons.

Assess the benefit capability of the long option that is staying in the exchange.

Now, what you have to decide is whether the fundamental security is probably going to move the correct way. If you possess a call contract, then you will trust that it climbs. Then again, you will foresee that it goes down if you possess a put option.

A Word on Volatility

Loads of books and sites talk about different option methodologies that are intended to profit by changes in instability. The majority of that is great, and well.
There is no contending that instability should be observed intently, however when the premiums make the diagonal spread ugly, it's a smart thought to get your work done first before entering a situation for the following couple months.

Chapter 5: Designing a trading plan

You need to have a long-term plan of success that will serve as your reference guide, as well as a business plan.

Trading Plans

You'll hear a lot of trading gurus tell you to make a plan. Well, what exactly is a trading plan, and why do you need one? To be honest, a trading plan by itself is not going to matter too much. However, when done right, it can help you focus and really nail down your vision when it comes to trading.

Perhaps a more appropriate term for this is to call it a trading business plan instead of just a trading plan. Much like how you need to record all key information (both financial and in terms of vision) in your business plan, your trading plan needs to do the same for your trading business. At a minimum, it needs to have the following information.

Instruments to Trade

What instruments will you be trading? List them all out here. You can even take this a step further and list out the individual stocks you will be trading. When starting out, it's best to pick a single instrument and trade just that. The methods described in this book work for any instrument on any time frame.

This doesn't mean you go out and try to trade everything under the sun. You build a base with one, then two instruments, and then expand outward. Much like individuals, stocks have natures of their own in terms of liquidity and volatility. Some stocks have certain tendencies, depending on the time of the day.

You need to observe and learn all this in order to trade successfully and doing so one by one is the way to go about it.

Markets and Timing

Which markets will you be trading? When will you trade them? Most of you reading this book will have full-time jobs or something else going on. So, it is important for you to note down your session time and stick to it.

Which is the best session for beginners or busy people to trade? Well, there's no such thing as "best" to begin with. In terms of liquidity and best bang for your buck, the open is probably the best. The flip side to this is that the volatility can be pretty extreme. Things pick up toward the end of the day as well, so it's not as if the open is the only worthwhile time to trade.

The afternoon session is usually seen as something of a graveyard with a lot of traders stepping out for lunch. Don't just assume this is so. Observe the market and check its tendencies. While the more active stocks tend to slow down quite a bit, there are some instruments that provide easy pickings.

Risk Limits

What is your daily risk limit? Weekly, monthly, etc.? It is also a good idea to execute a gain-protection plan. What this means is that if you have a bunch of winners during the session (say two or more) or if you make a certain percentage of your account during the session (say anything about 0.5%), then you could decide to stop trading during that session if your gains dip below 0.25% or if you lose two more trades.

The idea is that you've made money during the session and you would like to hang on to it. This is to protect a string of winners or a huge gain. Once you've had a great day, it's perfectly fine to set a lower loss limit in order to protect some of it so that no matter what happens, you'll end the day up.

Events

The markets have a bunch of external events that affect them, such as earnings announcements, dividends, splits, interest rate announcements, press conferences, and on and on. Generally speaking, you need to pay attention to the following events:

- earnings
- special events pertaining to the individual stock or political events like elections
- interest rate announcements
- nonfarm payrolls (NFP)

That's it. These events are always scheduled in advance, and as a beginner, stop trading an hour prior to the announcement and resume an hour after it has passed. The reason is that volatility jumps like crazy, and your stops will get triggered.

If you have any positions open that are close to profit, take a lower profit just before the announcement, as long as it doesn't affect your risk numbers too much. Similarly, if you have a trade that is in a loss and is near its stop-loss, you have to close the trade out just before the event.

If your trade is in the middle of the road or is even break even, ride the event out and hope for the best. Some stocks are better than others in this regard. Stay away from flashy companies run by Twitter-wielding CEOs who tend to send their products into space instead of building profits. You know who I'm talking about.

Aside from being annoying, you can bet there will be a number of algorithms and bots tracking every character such people type into Twitter, and all it takes for a flash tumble to occur in the stock is a typo or a rash tweet. Stick to boring names no one has heard of, and you'll be much better off, no matter how much you love or hate the company.

Review System

Every successful trader spends a lot of time reviewing their trades and actions over the week. Mention the time you will spend reviewing.

Practice

When will you practice your skills? What skills will you practice? Each strategy has a number of skills you need to execute, not to mention mental skills. Set aside time to practice each of these individually in order to perfect it.

Journals

As important as your trading plan is, the document that is of primary importance for your trading success is your trading journal. This will list all the trades you took over the past week and serve as a record for you to review. In addition to written records, you should also save screenshots of your trades on entry and exit.

Remember also to save screenshots of the market condition on the higher time frame on trade entry. Many times, on review, you will notice how you might have misjudged the higher time frame action. Below are the things your trading journal needs to record at a minimum:

- Date
- Instrument (the ticker or name of the stock)
- Entry price
- Stop-loss level
- Stop distance

- Position size
- Reasons for entry (describe in as much detail why this entry was in line with your strategy and what you saw)
- Reasons or exit
- Exit date
- P/L
- Mental state on entry
- Mental state on exit

You can either have this recorded on a spreadsheet or in a notebook; it doesn't matter where as long as you can review it easily. Save your screenshots in a numbered manner and in appropriate folders. In addition to this, you can also record your screen and yourself during the session and review your demeanor and market action at the time of entry to verify whether you were seeing things correctly.

Remember, the more information you record at the time, the more potential things there are for you to improve and learn.

Aside from the trading journal, you should also keep a mental journal. This is simply a record of what your mental state was during the session and if anything was bothering you at the time. It's up to you as to how much information you want to put in here, but you must aim to record whether you followed your preparation routines properly on that particular day.

Your prep routine can include physical exercise, meditation, visualization, affirmations, skill practice, and so on. It's up to you to decide what you want to include. Your aim should be to include things that are as repeatable as possible. Don't include too many things because you like the idea of it but will be stretched for time when it comes to implementing it.

The last journal you need to have is a review journal. You can incorporate this within your trade journal itself or as a separate document. When you're starting out, if it is logistically possible, I'd recommend reviewing your session after a 30-minute break once it ends. This way, the action is still fresh in your mind, and you're more relaxed.

Go through all your trades and review the screenshots. Review the video recording as well to confirm and check if what you saw was true. Record what you did incorrectly and, even more importantly, record what you did right. The review is not just about finding things to improve; it's also to celebrate things you did right.

Doing a review after each trading session will increase your rate on improvement as opposed to doing it weekly. Remember, even a session where you place no trades should be reviewed for mental state and whether you were tuned in or zoned out. Did you miss any opportunities? Leave no stone unturned.

Training

Trading is a unique endeavor in that we spend more time in the market (that is, game day) than in practice. Every other high-performance activity requires a minimum of double the amount of time to be spent in practice than in games. So how do you achieve this when it comes to trading?

Well, first off, you're not going to be able to achieve anything like double the amount of practice time as trading time. However, by simply assigning time every day to practice and improve your skills and strategy, you'll be putting yourself way ahead of the curve.

Schedule at least 15 minutes every day to train your skills on simulation. Break down your strategy into its individual elements and practice each skill separately. Another thing you can commit to is to practice your skills in session if it happens to be slow or if there aren't any opportunities available.

Simulation software has a market replay feature, so you can simulate a market at a much faster pace and really hone your skills instead of letting dead market time go to waste. Finally, schedule a month off each year or a couple of weeks off every quarter to review your existing skill set and to improve yourself as a trader.

Remember, do not trade every single day that the market is open. This is the easiest way to go insane. Take some time off and schedule breaks to keep yourself fresh.

Progression

How should you build your skill set? Well, your progression should always be from simulation to demo and only then to live. You need to place at least 200 trades on demo and make money from the demo before going live. It simply isn't worth it otherwise. Your practice should be done on simulation software to ensure you're keeping your skills fresh.

Once you've successfully completed 200 trades on demo and have made money on the instrument, you then add the next instrument on simulation and back-test your strategy on it. Once this pass, you demo trade it for 200 trades. Once you make money on this, you begin trading it live.

Chapter 6: Trading Psychology

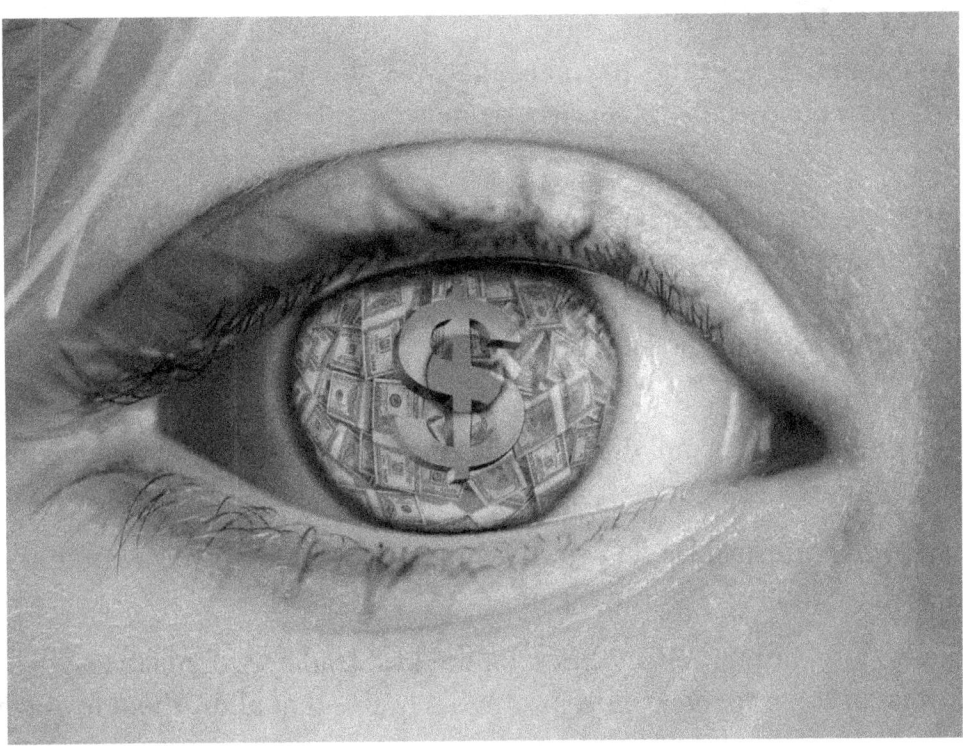

We associate trading psychology to some behaviors and emotions that are often the triggers for catalysts for decisions. The most common emotions that every trader will come across is fear and greed.

Fear

At any given time, fear represents one of the worst kinds of emotions that you can have. Check in your newspaper one day, and you read about a steep selloff, and the next thing is trying to rack your brain about what to do next even if it isn't the right action at that time.

Many investors think that they know what will happen in the next few days, which makes them have a lot of confidence in the outcome of the trade. This leads to investors getting into the trade at a level that is too high or too low, which in turn makes them react emotionally.

As the trader puts a lot of hope on the single trade, the level of fear tends to increase, and hesitation and caution kick in.

Fear is part of every trader, but skilled traders have the capacity to manage the fear. There are various types of fears that you will experience, let us look at a few of them:

The Fear to Lose

Have you ever entered a trade and all you could think about is losing? The fear of losing makes it hard for you to execute the perfect strategy or enter or exit a strategy at the right time.

As a trader, you know that you need to make timely decisions when the strategy signals you to take one. When fear is guiding you, the level of confidence drops, and you don't have the ability to execute the strategy the right way, at the right time. When a strategy fails, you lose trust in your abilities as well as strategy.

When you lose trust in many of the strategies, you end up with analysis paralysis, whereby you don't have the capacity to pull the trigger on any decision that you make. Making a move becomes a huge challenge.

When you cannot pull the trigger, all you can think about is staying away from the pain of losing, while you need to move towards gains.

No trader likes to lose, but it is a fact that even the best traders will make losses once in a while. The key is for them to make more profitable trades that allow them to stay in the game.

When you worry too much, you end up being distracted from your execution process, and instead, you focus on the results.

To reduce the fear in trading, you need to accept losses. The probability of losing or making a profit is 50/50, and you need to accept this fact and accept a trade, whether it is a sell or a buy signal.

The Fear of a Positive Trend Going Negative (and Vice Versa)

Many traders choose to go for quick profits and then leave the losses to run down. Many traders want to convince themselves that they have made some money for the day, so they tend to go for a quick profit so that they have the winning feeling.

So, what should you do instead? You need to stick with the trend. When you notice a trend is starting, it is good to stay with the trend until you have a signal that the trend is about to reverse. It is only then that you exit this position.

To understand this concept, you need to consider the history of the market. History is good at pointing out that times change, and trends can go either way. Remember that no one knows the exact time the trend will start or end; all you need to do is wait upon the signal.

The Fear of Missing Out

For every trade, you have people that doubt the capacity of the trade to go through. After you place the trade, you will be faced with many skeptics that will doubt the whole procedure and leave you wondering whether to exit the strategy or not.

This fear is also characterized by greed – because you aren't working on the premise of making a successful trade rather the fact that the security is rising without you having a piece of the pie.

This fear is usually based on information that there is a trend which you missed that you would have capitalized on.

This fear has a downside – you will forget about any potential risk associated with the trade and instead think that you have the capacity to make a profit because other people benefited from the action.

Fear of Being Wrong

Many traders put too much emphasis on being right that they forget that this is a business they should run the right way. They also forget that being successful is all about knowing the trend and how it affects their engagement.

When you follow the best timing strategy, you create many positive results over a certain time.

The uncanny desire to focus on always being right instead of focusing on making money is a great part of your ego, and to stay on the right path; you need to trade without your ego for once.

If you accommodate a perfectionist mentality when you get into trades, you will be after failure because you will experience a lot of losses as well. Perfectionists don't take losses the right way, and this translates into fear.

Ways to Overcome Fear in Trading

As you can see, it is obvious that fear can lead to losses. So, how can you avoid this fear and become successful?

- Learn

You need to find a way to get knowledge so that you have the basis for making decisions. When you know all there is to know about options, you know what to buy and when to sell, and learn which ones to watch. You are then more comfortable making the right decisions.

- Have Goals

What are your short term and long-term goals? Setting the right goals helps you to overcome fear. When you have goals, you have rules that dictate how you behave, even in times of fear. You also have a timeline for your journey.

- Envision the Bigger Picture

You always need to evaluate your choices at all times and see what you have gained or lost so far for taking some steps. Understanding the mistakes, you made gives you guidance to make better decisions in the future.

- Start Small

Many traders that subscribe to fear have lost a lot before. They put a lot of funds on the line and ended up losing, which in turn made them fear to place other trades. Begin with small sums so that you don't risk too much to put fear in you. Once you get more confident, you can invest larger sums so that you enjoy more profit.

- Use the Right Strategy

Having the right trading strategy makes it easy to execute your trades successfully. Make sure you look at various options trading strategies so that you know which one is ideal for your situation and skills.

Many strategies can help you succeed, but others might leave you confused. If you have a strategy that doesn't give you the returns you desire, then adjust it to suit your needs over time. Refine it till you are comfortable with its performance.

- Go Simple

When you have a strategy that is simple and straightforward, you will be less likely to lose confidence along the way because you know what to expect.

Additionally, the easier the strategy, the faster it will be to spot any issues.

- Don't Hesitate

At times you have to jump into the fray even if you aren't so comfortable with the way it works. Once you begin taking steps, you will learn more about the trade.

However, you need always to be prepared when taking any trade. The more prepared you are, the easier it will be for you to run successful trades.

- Don't Give Up

Things might not always go as you expect them to do. Remember that mistakes are there to give you lessons that will make you a better trader. When you lose, take time to identify the mistake you made and then correct it, then try again.

Greed

This refers to a selfish desire to get more money than you need from a trade. When the desire to get more than you can usually make takes over your decision-making process, you are looking at failure.

Greed is seen to be more detrimental than fear. Yes, fear can make you lose trades, but the good thing is that you get to preserve your capital. On the other hand, greed places you in a situation where you spend your capital faster than you return it. It pushes you to act when you shouldn't be acting at all.

The Danger of Being Greedy

When you are greedy, you end up acting irrationally. Irrational trading behavior can be overtrading, overleveraging, holding onto trades for too long, or chasing different markets.

The more greed you have, the more foolish you act. If you reach a point at which greed takes over from common sense, then you are overdoing it.

When you are greedy, you also end up risking way much more than you can handle, and you end up with a loss. You also have unrealistic expectations from the market, which makes it seem as if you are after just money and nothing else.

When you are greedy, you also start trading prematurely without any knowledge of the options trading market.

When you are too greedy, your judgment is clouded, and you won't think about any negative consequences that might result when you make certain decisions.

Many traders that were too greedy ended up giving up after making this mistake in the initial trading phase.

How to Overcome Greed

Like any other endeavors in trading, you need a lot of efforts to overcome greed. It might not be easy because we are talking about human emotions here, but it is possible.

First, you have to know that every call you make won't be the right one at all times. There are times when you won't make the right move, and you will end up losing money. At times you will miss the perfect strategy altogether, and you won't move a step ahead.

Secondly, you have to agree that the market is way bigger than you. When you do this, you will accept and make mistakes in the process.

Hope

Hope is what keeps a trading expectation alive when it has reached reversal. Hope is usually factored in the mind of a trader that has placed a huge amount on a trade. Many traders also go for hope when they wish to recoup past losses. These traders are always hopeful that the next trade will be the best, and they end up placing more than they should on the trade.

This type of emotion is dangerous because the market doesn't care at all about your hopes and will take your money.

Regret

This is the feeling of disappointment or sadness over a trade that has been done, especially when it has resulted in a loss.

Focusing too much on missing on trade makes the trader not to move forward. After you learn the lessons after such a loss, you need to understand the mistakes you made then move ahead.

Chapter 7: Risk Management

What Is Money Management?

Money management is how you handle your finances, your savings, your expenditure, and investments. It is making sure you can survive a financial crisis. It means planning a budget for your long-term goals and also making investments that will help you to achieve your goals successfully. When you manage your money, you will be able to make wise purchases. Otherwise, you will always complain of having less amount of money no matter how much your income is. It can also be known as investment management.

Money management is more about risk. When you have better money management skills, you will reduce the risk. You must understand all the areas of money management to be able to avoid any risks. Plan with a negative bias, always ask yourself "what-if" scenarios, take action, and plan. When budgeting for money management, make sure you are spending less than what you save. Excellent money management will help you monitor your spending before going beyond your budget. By doing this, you will secure your savings.

You will be able to invest if you make the right decisions. Avoiding taking on more risks will help you reach your financial goals. The strategies you use in your investments play a significant role in your success. When you decide to invest, the first important thing to focus on is the risk involved, and you can avoid it. Here are some of the basics, advantages, and disadvantages of money management.

The Basics of Money Management

Money management is a wide term that involves solutions and services in the entire investment industry. You can now have a wide range of resources in today's market and also phone applications to help you manage all your finances. Investors can also seek services from a financial advisor for professional money management. Financial advisors work with private banking and even brokerage services to offer money management plans involving services like retirement and estate planning.

The Advantages of Money Management

Better tracking of your money. When you have a reasonable budgeting plan, you can track how you use your money, and you can monitor every expense. This is a significant benefit to you, as you can spend less and end up saving more money. Monitor your expenses for some months and then change your budgeting by removing the less required expense and allocate that money to your savings plan, a retirement plan, or a vacation fund. Excellent money management will help you stay on track; you will be able to pay your bills on time, will be able to stay within your limit, and avoid bank account overdraws. Poor money management can put you in bad debt quicker than a blink of an eye. You can prevent those nasty fees charges when you go over your limit. By having an excellent budgeting plan, you will avoid overspending.

A good retirement plans. Better money management and savings plans will help you in the long term. You will be able to secure your future and have an excellent retirement plan. With better money management skills will give you a better retirement plan for you. No matter how much you save, even when you save and invest a small amount of money, it will provide you with a more significant amount for your retirement later in life.

Peace of mind. Proper money management brings you peace of mind. Having bills on the counter and having no idea on how you will pay the bills or not having the money to purchase something that you needed. All these issues can be difficult to face each day. Managing your money wisely and experience all the benefits of sound money management, you will enjoy peace of mind, and you can provide for yourself and your family, too.

The Disadvantages of Money management

Rapid changes. With the rapid changes in the financial world, it is required to change your management plans every time. It is sometimes challenging to adjust your planning to incorporate the fast-changing situations. Unless your plan can help to adopt the new techniques, it will be limited.

Time-consuming. Managing your money can sometimes be a time-consuming exercise. It requires you to make the estimates as accurate as possible. However, you can use software and mobile applications to assist you with planning, and this may reduce the time you will take if you were not using the technologies. And if you have less knowledge about money management, it will take you more time to achieve this.

Inaccuracy. When planning, you make a lot of assumptions in terms of estimation of your expenses. Any shift like economic downturn or the change in the currency rate or interest rates can change your estimates in your planning.

What Are Money Skills?

People giving out money advice sometimes overcomplicates things. Some myths make it harder to save money and be rich, so try to forget about them. Also, some of the tips available are overwhelming and seem unnecessary. Most successful people can balance their check without a business degree or any financial training. However, you can get by with basic information about excellent money skills.

What are these money skills that everyone should know about? Don't try to memorize all the rules. Try to understand each one of them and implement them in your day-to-day life. I will list down some money skills that will set you up on a path to financial freedom.

Budget without "budgeting". Budgeting may seem like a basic thing, but it is arguably not. Only a few households keep a detailed budget. This is critical behavior, mainly if you are not hitting your primary goals—for example, fully funding your emergency fund. Luckily, you can use tools like Excel sheets and other software that are tailor-made for different personalities and requirements. Is staying disciplined in your budgeting and spending a problem for you? Consider the envelope method. From the name, this method involves having physical envelopes for your expenses and keep your cash in. This method can help you to reset your mind's bad habits. Budgeting is a process, and once your savings start to grow, you can switch to auto-deposits.

Manage debt with clear eyes. Not all debts are equal. There is student debt, which you can pay off by the increase in your income. Getting a mortgage is cheaper than renting. Some of these debts can be an investment in the future; however, you still have to make a plan for tackling these debts.

There are two methods of paying off your debts, and both ways use snow metaphors. One of the methods is the avalanche approach, where you start with the highest-interest debts first. The other one is the snowball approach, where you start with the smallest and easiest debts to pay off first. The avalanche method is usually the best to choose in terms of saving. Let's say you have $43,000 of debts of car loans, student debt, and credit card debt. When you use the avalanche method, you will end up saving up to over $1,000 a month sooner on interest payments. However, the snowball method is also appealing. If small victories keep you going, then you can consider choosing this method. It all depends on your personality.

Have a written plan. Financial freedom is a choice. The financial decision you make today will determine how close or far you are moving from your financial goals. Write down a financial goals plan, and this plan will guide you throughout your journey to financial success. The written plan is not about writing down some motivation words through your plans. Instead, write more detailed information defining every aspect of your financial goals and include illustrations and exact words and figures. Define your timeline and quantum of your money management to achieve your financial goals.

Start right away. Start your savings earlier to be able to achieve your financial success and start planning your retirement. You don't have to be a financial guru to begin. With early savings, you will have enough time to grow your savings rate.

Don't touch your social security. Do not tap into your social security no matter what urgent your need is as social security should be the last option. Social security is to be used after your retirement, and this means you might meet your daily expenses with your social security amount. Your pension would be better if you wait longer before you claim your social security.

Plan your risks. The higher the risk, the higher your returns will be. However, this doesn't mean you should rush into a high-risk investment with thinking twice. Based on someone's financial status, each person can afford to take risks differently. So, you need to evaluate your financial situation and if you can handle a loss financially. By doing this, you will have a clear image of the risk you can afford to handle. Capital preservation should be your top priority when planning for your retirement. Access your risk profile before investing.

Plan your taxes. Between your income, expenditures, and savings, one compulsory factor is taxes. As a citizen of a country, you should be familiar with the taxation laws and how your income is taxed. Use your knowledge of tax planning and try to save more on your funds. Learning Tax planning will help you when you retire, you will be able to handle your investments which are liable to be taxed carefully.

Apply the 5% rule. This is a beneficial and practical rule. It merely means that you cut down on your expenses by 5% from your top 3 expenses in your categories yearly. To be able to apply this skill, you first have to list down your top 3 expenses in your categories, then break them down within the categories, and by doing this, you will know which areas you can save money on. For example, dining out is part of your monthly expenses, and this is essential to make it to your list. You can quickly achieve your financial goals by breaking down into habits and creating good savings habits.

Why Is Money Management Important?

Money turns to wealth when it is well-managed. It is an instrument which is used to pursue wealth. For wealthy people, having and spending money does not bring them happiness, which gives them joy is having a steady income, and they can go on achieving their goals— and being able to leave a legacy to their loved ones. Money management focuses on your habits, and your decision making can have affected the outcome in your long-term strategies. In pursuit of wealth, there are many powerful elements such as debts, risks, and taxes that can take away all the hard work you have put in to achieve your goals. This is a life skill that everyone must learn. You don't have to be financially savvy to start managing your money. There is plenty of information available to help you better understand your finances. The following are the importance of money management.

Chapter 8: Trading as a Business

Options trading is flexible. You don't have to dive into options trading full time if you don't want to. You can do it very part-time, and set a goal of only making a few hundred dollars a month, or you can go full-fledged into options trading and try and build a million dollar a year business.

Trading as a business can, but doesn't necessarily have to, mean setting up an actual business for your trading activities. Depending on the laws of your location, you can setup a corporate entity and use that for your trading activities. Approaching it in that way will require satisfying all of the legal requirements, including tax forms, and setting up separate bank accounts. This is not an accounting book or one that provides legal advice, so please check with an accountant for details.

Of course, it is not necessary to setup a business for options trading. You can certainly do it and just treat it as individual income. Keep in mind that options trading – for the most part – is going to involve short term capital gains. In the United States short term capital gains are treated as regular income for tax purposes. If you do invest in LEAPs and hold some assets for a year or longer, you may be able to treat your gains as long-term capital gains, and get preferential tax treatment.

You are unlikely to run into any legal trouble with the one exception being opening a margin account. If you open a margin account and are unable to meet your debt obligations, then you could get into some trouble. That might be something to consider when thinking about whether or not you start your trading activities as an official business to separate it from your personal activities. But for most people it shouldn't be necessary to go through all the trouble of setting up a business when it comes to options trading.

One of the most important things to get a handle on when you begin trading options is a plan for risk management. On the losing side, this means having a "stop loss". That is a value you use to determine when to exit a trade. So, if the options price were to drop say $50, you can setup your trading platform to automatically sell any options that fit this description. Alternatively, you can also setup trades to automatically sell when you reach a certain level of profit. This is called a "take profit". Check to see if your trading platform allows you to enter automatic stop loss and take profit orders.

If you can, this will greatly simplify your trading activities, and keep you from making impulsive and emotional mistakes. Instead, you will be able to cap your losses on any given trade, and ensure that if stock prices are rising, you get out with profits without waiting too long because you get excited and greedy. Remember, that can lead to losses. It is better to put caps, which of course means that you are going to miss out on some gains from time to time. But more often than not, it means that you are going to avoid making large mistakes. It is better to consistently make $50 profits, rather than holding on too long all the time hoping to score big and ending up with small profits or even losses.

If your system does not allow you to enter automatic stop loss and take profit orders, you are going to have to develop some personal discipline and manage those manually. That means that you would have to pay attention to your gains and losses, and be ready to exit trades when the rule you have decided upon is realized.

There are no hard rules to follow, you will have to pick something that works for you. But in my opinion, on a per option basis, a maximum loss of $25 is reasonable. So, if you enter into a trade and you are losing $25 per options contract, you should go ahead and sell your options. This is a matter of cutting losses without letting them get out of control while you hope that things get better. Also, it will keep you from panicking too easily, by setting a fairly significant loss level, you will keep yourself from jumping out too early when the stock is going to reverse and make profits for your options.

On the other side, for take profit, take a 2-to-1 to 4-to-1 ratio. So, if you are going to have a $25 stop loss limit, then set your take profit to $50, or possibly $100, per options contract or trade.

These rules are not going to guarantee profits. Sometimes they are going to work to provide winning trades, and sometimes this is not going to appear to help you. What you are looking for is a systematic approach that will help you to earn profits on average. The specific values you pick are less important than simply having some kind of risk management system. Of course, you don't want to be too conservative, because then you will be missing out on a lot of profits and getting out of many trades too early.

And don't stop here. Remember that we said you should be aiming to educate yourself as an options trader continually. So, get online and find out what other options traders are doing, and settle on the type of risk management system that fits you the best. Remember that different traders are going to have different levels of risk tolerance.

Professional traders often use a set of tools known as technical analysis in order to help them make better trades. Specifically, technical analysis can help you detect developing trend reversals in stock charts, and this information can help you get into and out of your trades at the best possible time. Technical analysis is a favorite tool of day and swing traders, and some options traders use it, but not all options traders do. Nonetheless, you should have some familiarity with it to determine if it is something you feel could help your trading.

Technical analysis involves a wide range of tools. These include looking at moving averages and specialized types of charts known as candlestick charts. Some traders also look for stock chart patterns that can signify a trend reversal, or change in price momentum.

It's important not to get too enamored with technical analysis. That is, you don't want to get into a mindset where you view technical analysis as "fact", because the cold truth about technical analysis is that it is a tool and nothing more. It is too easy to put far too much faith into technical analysis that really isn't deserved. Nonetheless, technical analysis is definitely a useful tool, and you can pick and choose specific tools of the trade that you feel will help you make more educated trading decisions. In this chapter I will briefly review the trading tools that I personally believe are the best ones to use when trying to find the best times to get in and out of options trades.

The most important thing on a stock chart that a trader is going to look for on a stock chart is a trend reversal. If you are looking to profit from call options, then what you are going to look for is a relatively low stock price, or a stock price that is in decline, and then wait for it to show signs of a reversal. In other words, this is going to help you buy low, and sell high. So, the technique once you have entered a position is to study the charts looking for the coming reversal once the price has peaked, and so you can exit your position.

Moving averages are the easiest tools to use for this purpose. What a moving average does is it takes several time periods of stock data, and at each point, it calculates the average, out to a fixed number of points. The definition of a "point" is up to the individual trader, it could be an hour, a four-hour period, a day, or a week. It could even be five-minute intervals. If you are planning on trading an option over a 30-day period, then you will probably be looking at using days for your time frame. In that case, a 9-period moving average would calculate the average of the closing price at each day, using the past nine days to do the calculation.

In order to spot trend reversals, traders rely on using moving averages with different periods (but they will use the same definition of period, be it day, week, or five minutes). So, you could use a 9-period moving average, and a 20-period moving average. Alternatively, you might use a 50-period moving average, and a 200-period moving average.

Obviously a longer-period moving average is going to give you more information on the historical pricing level of the stock in question. Different types of moving averages are going to treat this in different ways. A simple moving average will do a standard mathematical average of all data points. So, if we had a 9-period simple moving average for closing prices of Apple, on a particular day it might calculate:

$$SMA = (212.41 + 213.11 + 212.50 + 214.29 + 215.72 + 216.01 + 217.22 + 217.50 + 216.95)/9$$

Many traders are completely content to use the simple moving average, but if you look at how it's calculated, you should note that all prices are treated the same. This is objectionable, because if you are looking to make a trade, recent prices are going to be more important to you than historical, older prices. We certainly want information from the historical pricing level of the stock, but it is more recent prices that are going to have the most impact on our trading decisions. For this reason, many traders use weighted moving averages, that give more weight to recent closing prices and less weight to closing prices in the past. There are two very popular weighted moving averages that are used, the Hull moving average, and the more popular exponential moving average.

In order to detect a trend reversal, you will use two moving averages on your stock chart of the same type, but with different period lengths. So, you can use a nine-day period exponential moving average with a 20-day period exponential moving average. No matter what type you choose and what periods you use, there are only two rules you need to worry about.

The first rule is known as a golden cross. This happens when the short-period moving average curve crosses above the long-period moving average curve. This tells you that the stock is likely to be entering an upward trend. In the example below, a 50-day simple moving average and a 200-day simple moving average are used. Notice that after the golden cross (the 50-day moving average crossing above the 200-day moving average), the stock enters into a relatively long-term upward trend.

Chapter 9: Technical Analysis

This analysis makes use of models and trading rules using different price and volume changes. These include the volume, price, and other different market info.

Technical analysis is applied among financial professionals and traders and is used by many option traders.

The Principles of Technical analysis

Many traders on the market use the price to come up with information that affects the decision you make ultimately. The analysis looks at the trading pattern and what information it offers you rather than looking at drivers such as news events, economic and fundamental events.

Price action usually tends to change every time because the investor leans towards a certain pattern, which in turn predicts trends and conditions.

Prices Determine Trends

Technical analysts know that the price in the market determines the trend of the market. The trend can be up, down, or move sideways.

History Usually Repeats Itself

Analysts believe that an investor repeats the behavior of the people that traded before them. The investor sentiment usually repeats itself. Due to the fact that the behavior repeats itself, traders know that using a price pattern can lead to predictions.

The investor uses the research to determine if the trend will continue or if the reversal will stop eventually and will anticipate a change when the charts show a lot of investor sentiment.

Combination with Other Analysis Methods

To make the most out of the technical analysis, you need to combine it with other charting methods on the market. You also need to use secondary data, such as sentiment analysis and indicators.

To achieve this, you need to go beyond pure technical analysis, and combine other market forecast methods in line with technical work. You can use technical analysis along with fundamental analysis to improve the performance of your portfolio.

You can also combine technical analysis with economics and quantitative analysis. For instance, you can use neural networks along with technical analysis to identify the relationships in the market. Other traders make use of technical analysis with astrology.

Other traders go for newspaper polls, sentiment indicators to come with deductions.

The Different Types of Charts Used in Technical Analysis

Candlestick Chart

This is a charting method that came from the Japanese. The method fills the interval between opening and closing prices to show a relationship. These candles use color coding to show the closing points. You will come across black, red, white, blue, or green candles to represent the closing point at any time.

Open-high-low-close Chart (OHLC)

These are also referred to as bar charts, and they give you a connection between the maximum and minimum prices in a trading period. They usually feature a tick on the left side to show the open price and one on the right to show the closing price.

Line Chart

This is a chart that maps the closing price values using a line segment.

Point and Figure Chart

This employs numerical filters that reference times without fully using the time to construct the chart.

Overlays

These are usually used on the main price charts and come in different ways:

- Resistance – refers to a price level that acts as the maximum level above the usual price
- Support – the opposite of resistance, and it shows as the lowest value of the price
- Trend line – this is a line that connects two troughs or peaks.
- Channel – refers to two trend lines that are parallel to each other

- Moving average – a kind of dynamic trendline that looks at the average price in the market
- Bollinger bands – these are charts that show the rate of volatility in a market.
- Pivot point – this refers to the average of the high, low, and closing price averages for a certain stock or currency.

Price-based Indicators

These analyze the price values of the market. These include:

- Advance decline line – this is an indicator of the market breadth
- Average directional index – shows the strength of a trend in the market
- Commodity channel index – helps you to identify cyclical trends in the market
- Relative strength index – this is a chart that shows you the strength of the price
- Moving average convergence (MACD) – this shows the point where two trend line converge or diverge.
- Stochastic oscillator – this shows the close position that has happened within the recent trading range
- Momentum – this is a chart that tells you how fast the price changes

Technical Analysis Secrets to Become the Best Trader

To make use of technical analysis the right way, you need to follow time-testing approaches that have made the technique a gold mine for many traders. Let us look at the various tips that will take you from novice to pro in just a few days:

Use More than One Indicator

Numbers make trading easy, but it also applies to the way you apply your techniques. For one, you need to know that just because one technical indicator is better than using one, applying a second indicator is better than using just one. The use of more than one indicator is one of the best ways to confirm a trend. It also increases the odds of being right.

As a trader, you will never be 100 percent right at all times, and you might even find that the odds are stashed against you when everything is plain to see. However, don't demand too much from your indicators such that you end up with analysis paralysis.

To achieve this, make use of indicators that complement each other rather than the ones that clash against each other.

Go for Multiple Time Frames

Using the same buy signal every day allows you to have confidence that the indicator is giving you all you need to know to trade. However, make sure you look for a way to use multiple timeframes to confirm a trend. When you have a doubt, it is wise that you increase the timeframe from an hour to a day or from a daily chart to a weekly chart.

Understand that No Indicator Measures Everything

You need to know that indicators are supposed to show how strong a trend is, they won't tell you much more. So, you need to understand and focus on what the indicator is supposed to communicate instead of working with assumptions.

Go with the Trend

If you notice that an option is trading upward, then go ahead and buy it. Conversely when the trend stops trending, then it is time to sell it. If you aren't sure of what is going on in the market at that time, then don't make a move.

However, waiting might make you lose profitable trades as opposed to trading. You also miss out on opportunities to create more capital.

Have the Right Skills

It really takes superior analytical capabilities and real skill to be successful at trading, just like any other endeavor. Many people think that it is hard to make money with options trading, but with the right approach, you can make extraordinary profits.

You need to learn and understand the various skills so that you know what the market seeks from you and how to achieve your goals.

Trade with a Purpose

Many traders go into options trading with the main aim of having a hobby. Well, this way you won't be able to make any money at all. What you need to do is to trade for the money – strive to make profits unlike those who try to make money as a hobby.

Always opt for High value

Well, no one tells you to trade any security that comes your way – it is purely a matter of choice. Try and go for high-value options so that you can trade them the right way. Make use of fundamental analysis to choose the best options to trade in.

Be Disciplined

When using technical analysis, you might find yourself in situations that require you to make a decision fast. To achieve success, you need to have strict risk management protocols. Don't base on your track record to come up with choices; instead, make sure you follow what the analysis tells you.

Don't Overlook Your Trading Plan

The trading plan is in place to guide you when things go awry. Coming up with the plan is easy, but many people find it hard to implement the plan the right way. The trading plan has various components – the signals and the take-profit/stop-loss rules. Once you get into the market, you need to control yourself because you have already taken a leap. Remember you cannot control the indicators once they start running – all you can do is to prevent yourself from messing up everything.

Come up with the trading rules when you are unemotional to try and mitigate the effects of making bad decisions.

Accept Losses

Many people trade with one thing in mind – losses aren't part of their plan. This is a huge mistake because you need to understand that every trade has two sides to it – a loss and a profit. Remember that the biggest mistake that leads to losses isn't anything to do with bad indicators rather using them the wrong way. Always have a stop-loss order when you trade to prevent loss of money.

Have a Target When You Trade

So, what do you plan to achieve today? Remember, trading is a way to grow your capital as opposed to saving. Options trading is a business that has probable outcomes that you get to estimate. When you make a profit, make sure you take some money from the table and then put it in a safe place.

How to Apply Technical Analysis

Many traders have heard of technical analysis, but they don't know how to use it to make deductions and come up with decisions that impact their trades. Here are the different steps to make sure you have the right decision when you use technical analysis.

Identify a Trend

You need to identify an option and then see whether there is a trend or not. The trend might be driving the options up or down. The market is bullish if it is moving up and bearish when it is moving down. As a trader, you need to go along with the trend instead of fighting it. When you fight against the trend, you incur unnecessary losses that will make it hard to achieve the rewards that you seek.

You also need to have good ways to identify the trend; this is because the market has the capacity to move in a certain direction. It is not all about identifying the direction of the trend but also when the trend is moving out of the trend.

So, how can you identify a trend the right way? Here are some tools to use so as to get the right trend:

- Using triangles that map major swings
- The Bill Williams Fractals indicator helps you to identify the trend
- Use the moving average
- Trend lines give you an idea of the direction of the trend

Once you identify the trend, the next step is to try and mark the support and resistance levels

Support and Resistance Levels

You need to understand the support and resistance levels that are within the trend. Use the Fibonacci retracement tool to identify these spots on the trend.

Look for Patterns

Patterns need to show you what to expect in a certain market. You can use candlesticks to determine the chart pattern.

Chapter 10: Searching for Trade

One of the main things you have to arrange for when you are preparing to exchange alternatives is actually how you are going to make your exchanges for example where will you purchase, sell, and compose alternatives. Most alternatives contracts are purchased and sold on different choices trades based the world over. These trades are effectively available to the overall population; however, you can't really complete the exchanges yourself. Similarly, you need the administrations of a stock dealer to purchase and sell stocks on the world's stock trades, you need an agent to purchase and sell choices.

On this page we clarify somewhat more about utilizing agents to exchange choices. We additionally take a gander at the two fundamental manners by which representatives can be characterized: full help or markdown, and on the web or disconnected.

Utilizing a Broker to Trade Options

Most stock intermediaries will complete choices exchanges for your sake, and there are likewise master choices agents who center explicitly around this specific budgetary instrument. Utilizing a merchant to exchange choices is exceptionally basic: you simply need to train them concerning what exchange you wish to complete and they will execute the exchange for you. Consequently, they will charge you a commission for every exchange, generally dependent on the size of the exchange in question.

There is a scope of various requests you can put with a representative, and these requests can be utilized to purchase contracts, sell existing agreements that you effectively own, and compose new agreements to sell. There are additionally sure specifications you can make as a major aspect of your requests, for example, least or most extreme costs to exchange at.

Picking an agent to use for exchanging alternatives can really be a troublesome choice, on the grounds that there are such a significant number of them. On the off chance that you as of now make ventures, in stocks and offers for instance, at that point you as of now have a record with an agent that can likewise be utilized to exchange alternatives. On the other hand, on the off chance that you have companions or relatives that you know utilize a dealer then you may wish to approach them for a suggestion.

Two Main Types of Brokers

The two principle sorts of representatives are full help agents and markdown intermediaries. The contrasts between the two are basically in the administrations that they offer and the expenses and commissions that they charge. Full assistance agents are normally the more costly of the two, since you will have an individual contact that will work with you on your speculations.

A decent full assistance specialist will set aside the effort to comprehend your own conditions and your speculation destinations, and afterward offer counsel and direction on what ventures you ought to make. Through a mix of recognizing what you are attempting to accomplish and their own insight and aptitude, they ought to have the option to assist you with arriving at your speculation objectives.

As you can envision, you do pay a premium for this degree of administration. On the off chance that you utilize a full assistance merchant, at that point you will typically pay genuinely high commissions on the entirety of your exchanges, and you might be dependent upon month to month or yearly charges as well.

Rebate merchants, as the name proposes, are generally less expensive and they offer limited commissions and charges. You will commonly pay fundamentally less commission for every exchange that you make and different expenses will be kept to a base. In any case, you won't advantage from having an expert help you with your speculations. A rebate intermediary is basically there to take your requests and execute them as needs be.

On the off chance that you have next to no speculation experience, at that point the benefits of a full help agent are genuinely clear. Be that as it may, the additional costs included shouldn't be disregarded. In the event that you are exchanging with generally small beginning capital, at that point utilizing a full assistance intermediary could genuinely affect upon your benefits. Likewise, on the off chance that you plan on being sensibly dynamic in your choices exchanging, at that point it may not be reasonable to look for exhortation before each exchange that you can make and, obviously, the more exchanges you are having the more effect the higher commissions will have.

As an exceptionally broad standard, we would prompt that rebate representatives are the better decision for choices dealers.

Online Brokers and Offline Brokers

Before, a financial specialist's relationship with their dealer would for the most part have been a generally close to home one. It was very typical for financial specialists, especially ordinary speculators, and their agents to realize each other sensibly well. The most well-known path for speculators to put orders with their representative would be via phone, and there was a lot of individual collaboration. While there are numerous speculators nowadays that despite everything have such associations with their dealers, the utilization of online agents is getting progressively far reaching.

Online intermediaries are commonly rebate specialists, so on the off chance that you would like to utilize a full help intermediary you might be in an ideal situation utilizing a disconnected representative that you can converse with via phone. Be that as it may, on the off chance that keeping expenses and commissions low is a need for you, at that point an online dealer is very likely the best decision for you. For most choices' dealers, we would recommend that utilizing an online specialist is a lot of the best approach, for various reasons.

The primary explanation we have just referenced; the cost investment funds can be very considerable when utilizing an online intermediary since you will regularly pay significantly less commission on every exchange you make. There will commonly be less to pay in the method of other record expenses as well, except if you explicitly need access to the different devices and extra administrations that some online representatives make accessible at an expense. The subsequent explanation is the simplicity of making exchanges. Utilizing an online specialist is fantastically basic once you become accustomed to the exchanging stage, and submitting choices requests is ordinarily simply an issue of making a couple of snaps of the mouse.

On the off chance that you will be generally dynamic when exchanging alternatives, at that point the capacity to put arranges rapidly is an immense preferred position. In the event that you are utilizing a day exchanging style, at that point a couple of moments contrast in getting your requests set and executed can now and then be the distinction between bringing in cash on an exchange and losing cash. Regardless of whether you aren't especially dynamic and just exchange periodically, the upsides of utilizing an online specialist presumably settle on this a superior decision than utilizing a disconnected intermediary.

Best Option Brokers for Beginners

Picking which intermediary to utilize when exchanging choices is without question one of the absolute most significant choices you will ever need to make in your exchanging profession. Utilizing a decent representative can set aside you cash, increment your productivity, spare you time, assist you with discovering exchanging openings, and it will for the most part improve your general exchanging experience.

Regardless of the significance of picking a specialist cautiously, numerous merchants join with any old intermediary and basically join the first they go over or the one that offers the best sign up impetus. Not placing any idea into what intermediary to utilize is a serious mix-up in light of the fact that, this truly is a choice that is well worth investing some energy in.

In the event that you are sufficiently fortunate to know an accomplished merchant that you confide in then asking them which intermediary they use is a decent method to locate a conventional agent, yet that isn't a strategy that is accessible to everybody. Then again, you could evaluate a scope of various intermediaries, look at them, and choose which one is best for you. In any case, this would be pretty tedious.

A choice is an agreement that permits (however doesn't require) a financial specialist to purchase or sell a basic instrument like a security, ETF or file at a specific cost over a specific timeframe.

How Brokers are Ranked

In the first place, we ought to likely clarify that there isn't generally any such thing as the "right" specialist from a general perspective. Choices merchants all have marginally various situations and somewhat various necessities and at last a ton is down to individual decision. A representative that is a decent decision for one dealer may not really be a decent decision for another merchant.

All things considered, we could never prescribe only one single representative to a wide crowd, however would prefer to furnish our peruses with a scope of recommendations and offer guidance on the most proficient method to choose the most appropriate. This is the reason we have grouped our suggestions into various classes.

Significant Factors to Consider Before Options Trading

While picking an intermediary you have to ponder which parts of an agent you should be mulling over. For tenderfoots and those hoping to make generally little exchanges, we accept that the accompanying components are especially significant and it's these that we propose you take a gander at when choosing which online choices representative to choose.

Generally, intermediaries could undoubtedly be put in one of two classes; they were either full assistance or markdown. The approach of online agents has made it fairly progressively hard to recognize the two as there will in general be much greater adaptability in the administrations advertised. Carefully, a full assistance specialist is one that will furnish you with proficient counsel and direction notwithstanding executing your requests for you while a rebate intermediary will essentially complete your requests as trained.

Nowadays various dealers can adequately be put in either, or both, of the classes as they offer a decision of administration to their clients. What you should choose is whether you need the extra administrations that are on offer, for example, accepting master guidance on potential exchanges and ventures, or whether you like to have a merchant that basically follows up on your guidelines. It won't shock you to realize that utilizing the extra administrations is the more costly alternative, and you will pay considerably less in commissions and charges when utilizing rebate administrations.

There's a thought coasting around that recommends apprentices are in an ideal situation utilizing a full assistance representative while they are as yet taking in and profiting by having an expert guide them as important. There are absolutely benefits in that game-plan, anyway we recommend that even apprentice choices brokers should utilize a markdown administration.

On the off chance that an alternate type of speculation was included, for example, putting resources into stocks and offers utilizing a purchase and hold technique, at that point the contentions for utilizing a full assistance agent would be more grounded in light of the fact that there are genuine advantages in having a specialist help you to design your ventures, find reasonable venture openings, and screen your portfolio.

Chapter 11: Day Trading Rules

All over the world, stock markets open in the morning. Those day traders who think they can start trading while munching on their breakfast, with no preparation, are among those who make losses. All businesses open in the morning. No successful business person just gets up, yawns and starts his business activities. Successful professionals arrive in their office with a clear idea of how they will tackle the work and related challenges. Likewise, to succeed in day trading, one must prepare beforehand. These preparations include many aspects; such as mental, physical, emotional, and financial.

Professional traders have clear advice for day traders; never trade if you are tired or stressed; never trade if you are feeling highly emotional, and trade with clear money management concepts. Day trading is a sophisticated business activity, where people try to earn money by using their intelligence. Therefore, physical or emotional stress can cause harm to your trading business. You will not be able to make rational decisions if you are tired or feeling stressed.

Before you start the day's trading, you should be physically, mentally and emotionally alert. A good night's sleep is necessary for traders to tackle the roller coaster ride of stock markets. Here are a few steps that will help you prepare for day trading with a cool temperament and calm mind.

Before going to sleep, keep your trading plan ready. Check the stock chart, make notes on the chart what big patterns the price created in the previous session. Note down the important support and resistance levels. Then mentally go over this chart and imagine how you will trade in the next session, in different trend conditions.

Do not spend too much time watching news about stock markets or anything else. Watching the news may create doubts in your mind about stock trends and influence your decision-making power for the next session. If possible, do some breathing exercises or meditation before going to sleep, which will sharpen your focusing power and reduce stress.

Also, prepare your money-plans for the next trading session. How much you will invest? What will be your loss tolerance level? And, what will be your profit booking point? During the trading hours, these decisions have to be made in a split second, and if you are already prepared, you will not hesitate to make the right decision. These will also help you set your goals for intraday trading. Just stick to your goals and you will not face any decision-making problems during the trading hours.

The final stage of your preparation will be an hour before the markets open in the morning. This is the time when you check the news reports about the business and financial world, and the economic calendar. By doing so, you will know what events could influence that day's trading pattern in the stock market. You can also check how the world markets are trading in that session. Sometimes all markets trade in one direction, which will be beneficial to know before your local stock markets open.

Planning for Trading

In day trading, financial instruments are bought and sold within the same session. Sometimes more than once through the same day. To be successful in this endeavor, traders need to know where the price might make important moves. Technical charts are very helpful tools in deciphering this price moment. Anybody involved in stock trading relies heavily on stock charts, which is why successful traders always create their trading plans before making any trading decisions.

When you create a trading plan, you are creating an 'assistant' to help you during the trading hours. This assistant will have all the information you will need for day trading; such as trade entry, trade exit, profit booking, stop loss and major price moments. Nobody goes looking for a treasure trove without any map. Likewise; no trader worth his or her salt will trade without a trading plan. Let us look at how a trading plan is created:

A trading plan is based on research, takes time, but saves a lot of effort and precious money during the trading hours. It is one of the most essential tools required for success in day trading. Every day trader has heard this saying 'fail to plan, and plan to fail'. Professional traders don't tire of emphasizing the importance of a trading plan. If you take their advice and prepare a trading plan before the markets open, you are halfway through to successful trading.

A trading plan is prepared before markets open and so, it is open to revisions and changes after markets start to trade and price changes. Every trader has a different trading style and based on that his trading plan could differ from others. But every trading plan must have a few essential details. These are:

1. Major support and resistance levels: One must mark the major support and resistance levels on the trading chart because these will symbolize the trade entry and exit points. These levels should be visible on charts to help in decision making during the chaotic trading hours.

2. Trade entry rules: Your trading plan should include when and why you will enter a trade. This could be a detailed explanation like 'if the price goes above X level, then buy'. Or it could be just a green arrow pointing to that price level.

3. Trade exit rules: Like the trade entry point, mark a trade exit or profit booking points on your trading plan. You must follow these rules meticulously, otherwise, these will become useless, if you plan and do not follow them.

4. Money management rules: Some traders like to note down on their trading plan, how much money they will invest in the next session. They keep checking their profits and losses through the session, and if the day's loss reaches its threshold; they stop trading. This is a good example of money discipline while trading because, in the excitement of trading, one can lose sight of what is happening with the investment capital.

These are the most basic rules to include in the trading plan. As you gain experience and get a hold of trading patterns in stock markets, you can expand your trading plans and include more trading rules in it. But always remember, these rules must be followed. A trading plan is based on research about markets, so every rule is important. Breaking any rule will be like going against the market, which is always harmful to any trader.

Chart Reading & Candlestick Charts

Day traders use different charts for technical analysis. The main types are line charts, bar charts, and candlestick charts. Some Forex traders also use Heiken Ashi and Ranko charts, but candlestick charts remain the most favorite of traders. The reason for this popularity is its simplicity. A green candlestick shows a positive price movement, and a red candlestick signals a fall in price. Day traders use various candlestick patterns to decipher the market trend.

The candlestick charts are more than a hundred years old. These were first used by Japanese rice traders to document the rise and fall in the rice prices. It was such an accurate system that stock traders also adopted it and it has since been a popular chart creating tool.

A single candlestick has two main parts; a body and a tail or wick. The body of the candlestick shows the opening and closing levels, while the wick shows the high and low marks. A green body shows that the price opened low but closed higher. And a red body shows higher open, but lower closing in that time frame. A single candlestick can be assigned to different time frames, ranging from one second to one month. These candlesticks make various patterns on charts. Traders try to decipher the price moment by how long the wick, or the body is, and how every candlestick is placed with other nearby candlesticks.

Candlestick charts are also used for automatic or algorithm trading, where buy and sell signals are generated by various patterns formed by candlesticks.

The up and down movement in stock prices creates candlesticks on charts. Sometimes, a single candlestick can indicate a trend reversal from high to low or low to high. These are called engulfing candlesticks and are so large that they completely engulf the previous candlestick. These can be both bullish and bearish candlesticks. A bullish candlestick is formed when the price-move creates a big positive or green candlestick, which overshadows the previous one. It signals that the price is ready to move higher and to start an uptrend.

Its opposite is a bearish engulfing candlestick pattern. Here, the stock price makes a big red candlestick overshadowing the previous one. This signals big selling pressure and shows that the price will fall further.

Another popular form of a candlestick is "Doji". Usually, this candlestick forms near the top or the bottom, after the price has made a long moment in either direction. In a Doji candlestick, the body is tiny, and the wicks are long. A small body denotes uncertainty in buyers and sellers; which shows that the market cannot decide whether to go up or down. Such an uncertain signal on top may indicate a trend reversal, and traders prepare for a fall in the market. A Doji formation at the bottom signals that the downtrend may come to an end and traders look for confirmation of a price-rise from lower levels.

Candlesticks create many types of patterns on a technical chart. This could involve a single or two or more candlesticks. There are many books about candlesticks and how to read candlestick charts. Traders who wish to know more about these charts, can read some of those books and enhance their knowledge.

Manage Your Time Effectively

Day trading is a demanding profession and requires significant time. Any market session runs for at least 6 hours a day, and you will have to spend that much time watching and observing markets; even if not reading. Apart from trading hours, a day trader needs to research, create trading plans, and keep learning new things. All these require time and effort.

Therefore; to succeed in day trading, you will need to manage your time effectively. Usually, people want to adopt a day trading career so they will have working flexibility. This means freedom from getting up early and rushing to get caught in the morning traffic, freedom from having a boss, and of course, financial freedom. Nothing comes easy in this world. A dream life also requires putting in lots of effort. Many day traders find it difficult to complete their trading routines; such as after-hours research and planning. Part-time traders who are already busy with some other work also struggle to prepare for day trading in their spare time.

With just a few adjustments, a day trader can find enough time to complete all steps required for a successful day trading.

Chapter 12: Option Strategies

Combination of Options

Combining options is a strategy that entails the sale and/or buying of both the put and call options on the same underlying asset. The following are some of the combinations available, starting with the two of the most popular ones:

Straddle

Straddle is a strategy that has unlimited profit potential and limited risk. Option traders usually make use of this strategy when they believe that the price of an underlying asset has the potential to make a strong move in both directions in the near future.

As an example, if an important court case is about to be decided, it can impact the stock price substantially, and in this situation, where the price's rise or fall isn't known beforehand makes straddle a good investment strategy. The biggest loss for this strategy is the both premiums (paid for the call and put).

Example:

Back in 2018, the options market was implying that AMD's stock was likely to rise or fall by 20% from the strike price at $26 for expiration on 16 November. Since buying one put and call cost $5.10, it put the stock in a trading range of between $20.90 and $31.15. One week later, the company's reports showed that the shares had plunged to $19.27 from $22.70 on 25th October. If you traded here with this strategy, you would have earned a profit since the stock fell outside the range, surpassing the premium cost of purchasing the calls and puts.

You can create a straddle scenario by purchasing an equal number of put options and at-the-money call with the same expiration date.

Strangle

Strangle just as the straddle is a strategy that also has the potential for unlimited profit with very limited risk. The only distinction between them is that out-of-the-money options are bought to create the strangle and, in the process, this lowers the cost of instituting a position. Nonetheless, a much superior move in the price of the underlying is necessary for this strategy to prove profitable.

Basically, as an investor, you can do a short strangle by selling an OTM put and OTM call. You however need to note that this approach is neutral and its profit potential is very limited. This means that trading in a short strangle will only profit you when the price of the stock trades in a narrow range between breakeven points.

Example

Let's assume company X's shares are trading at $50 per share. Using the strangle option strategy, you enter into two option positions: call and put. The call's strike is $52 and the premium here is $3; the total cost is $3 x 100 shares =$300.

The put option's strike price is $48 and the premium is $2.85, and its total cost is $2.85 x 100 shares = $285. Both options have a common date of expiry.

If the price of the stock remains at $48 - $52 over the lifespan of the option, your loss will be $585, which is the total cost of the two contracts.

However, if the company's stock becomes a bit volatile and the price of the shares ends up being $40, the call option will expire, and its loss will be $300. Nonetheless, the put has gained value and yields a profit of $715 (which is $1,000 less than the $285- the initial option cost). As a trader, your total gain therefore is $715- $300= $415.

If the price rises to $55, the put option will expire and the loss incurred will be $285. The profit brought by the call option is $500- $300 = $200. When you factor in the put option's loss, your trade will incur a loss of $200 - $285= -$85 since the price move wasn't large enough to compensate for the options' cost. Had the stock risen by $10 in price to $60 per share, the total gain would have been $1000- $300- $285 = $415

Other strategies you can also consider include the following:

Strap
This strategy is a more bullish variation of the straddle strategy. If you wish to modify a straddle into a strap, you need to purchase twice the number of call options.

Strip
Like the strap, the strip is also modified but it is a more bearish version of the basic straddle. You create it in a way that is similar to the straddle only that the ratio of calls to puts should be 1 to 2.

Synthetic underlying
Did you know that you could also use different combinations to construct option positions that have similar payoff patterns as the underlying stock? We refer to such positions as

synthetic underlying positions. Let us use equity options as an example in which you can create a synthetic long stock position by selling at-the-money options and buying an equal at-the-money-call.

Option Spreads

An option spread is a scenario that you can create when you simultaneously sell and buy options of the same underlying security and of the same class but with different expiration dates and/or strike prices. If you construct a spread using calls, then it will be known as a call spread. Equally, if you construct a spread using a put, it will be referred to as a put spread.

Significance of Options Spreads

As an option buyer, you should think about using options spreads since it decreases the net cost of joining a trade. Experienced option sellers use spreads to reduce the margin obligations so that they may free up purchasing power while simultaneously putting a cap on the highest loss probability.

Bear and Bull Spreads

A bull spread is a scenario when an option spread is constructed to profit from an increase in the price of an underlying security. On the other hand, a bear spread is an option spread where the favorable outcome is attained once the value of an underlying security decreases.

Debit and Credit Spreads

Option spreads can also be entered on either a net debit or net credit. If the premiums of the options that have been sold are more than the premiums of the purchased options, a net credit is acquired when joining the spread. The reverse is also true if a debit is taken. A spread that is entered on a credit is known as a credit spread while one entered on debit is known as a debit spread.

Using the information, we have so far, it is relatively straightforward to establish a bull put spread- all you need to do is sell one put option or short put while purchasing another put option or long put simultaneously

In April, you believe that stock X that is trading at $33 per share will increase over the following month moderately to $35 per share (or more), and you decide to initiate a bull put spread.

You purchase one X May 30 put for a premium of $2.60, and pay $260, since each contract covers 100 shares. Simultaneously, you sell one X May 32 put for a limit price of $3.50, and thus receive $350. The breakeven here is $31.10 (the highest strike price less the received premium). You should note that the put bought in this example is out of money and the put sold is a bit out of the money. The stock could rise or remain the same, or reduce a bit and still stay profitable. The maximum profit is the credit received for the trade which is $350-$260 = $90, less all the commission costs.

The maximum risk here is the difference between both strike prices, less the credit you received, which is $200- $90 =$110.

Mildly Bearish

This is an option strategy that will still make you money on condition that the price of the underlying stock does not increase on the options expiry date. A mildly bearish strategy will generally offer you a small upside protection as well.

This strategy will often provide a tiny upside protection too. A great example of a mildly bearish strategy is writing out-of-the-money naked calls.

This strategy involves writing OTM call options without owning an underlying stock, and it's often employed when the trader is neutral or mildly bearish on the underlying stock. Its objective is collecting the premiums when your options expire worthlessly.

You would write this call every month and if the stock remains flat or drops, you would take home the premiums and repeat the process as long as you perceive the market to stay the same.

Example:

Stock X is trading at $48. You decide to write a July 50 out-of-the-money naked call for $3, and thus get $300 for writing the call option. When the expiration date arrives, the stock rallies to $68. Given that $50 striking price for the call option is less than the trading price at the moment, the call gets assigned and you buy the shares for $6,800 and sell it at $5,000 to the options holder, which is essentially a loss of $1,800. Nonetheless, since you had received $300, your net loss is $1,500.

But what if the stock price goes down to $28 (20 points instead)? Let's see.

This means that the call expires worthless and you, the naked call writer, keeps the $300 in premiums received as profit. As you can see in the profit graph, you can see that the break-even is clearly at $53 (call strike + premium). As long as the stock price stays at $53 or lower, the writer doesn't experience any loss.

Very Bullish

The only option trading strategy, which is the most bullish is the basic Call purchasing strategy, which is one of the most preferred by apprentice options traders.

Example:

The bullish options strategy can generally be illustrated best with a technique that has a neutral to moderate market outlook known as covered call.

A covered call basically involves going short or selling a call option, but with a twist. As a trader, you sell a call but also purchase the option's underlying stock, 100 shares for every sold call. Owning the stock thus turns the short call, which is potentially risky, into a relatively safe trade able to generate income. As a trader, you expect the stock price to go below the strike price at expiration. If the stock completes above the strike price, you, the owner, has to sell the stock at the strike to the call buyer.

Let's take a simple example:

Stock X trades for $20 per share. A call with a $20 strike price and a four –month expiry period trades at $1. The contract pays a premium of $100. You buy 100 shares of the stock for $2000 and then sell one call to get $100.

The profit here is as follows:

You break even at $19 per share. You would lose money under $19 since the stock would lose money, more than having to offset the premium of $1. At $20, you would pocket the full premium and still hang on to the stock as well. Beyond $20, the gain gets capped at $100. Even though the short call loses $100 for each dollar that is increased over $20, the stock's gain offsets it fully, which leaves you with the initial premium of $100 received as the full profit.

Chapter 13: What is Forex

On the whole, the FOREX market functions like any other financial market. You have a series of buyers and sellers who are looking to make a profit buying and selling currency. In these transactions, you hope to buy at a lower price while hoping to sell at a higher price. That's really all there is to it in terms of the day-to-day transactions that you will be making.

Beyond that, the intricacies of the FOREX market are based upon the currencies you are dealing with. In short, you are pitting one country's currency against another countries. This is why you need to be aware of the economic, political, and social issues that influence the value of a nation's currency. As such, this understanding will help you figure out how you can spot a potential profit.

Thus, to make a profit, you need to be cognizant of how the value of a currency is determined.

The value of a currency is set by the market. However, it's important to note that there needs to be a second currency that can express the value of the first. It's like establishing the price of a pair of shoes. You need to use currency in order to express the value of the shoes. Otherwise, it's impossible to determine the price. Sure, you could express it in terms or sugar, automobiles or bottles of water, but that would be impractical.

The value of a currency is set just like any other commodity, that is, through the market. The market is what enables a currency to have a specific market value. In general, this market value is expressed in US Dollars as the US Dollar is the world reserve currency. Nevertheless, it is possible to express currencies in terms of any other currency. However, this can be a complex calculation, and it almost always involves pegging one currency to the US Dollar unless there is a specific calculation done among currencies. This is generally done among neighboring countries, especially when there is a large amount of trade among them.

Currency Pairs

FOREX is based on currency pairs. This means that you can only trade two currencies at any one time. While it is entirely possible to place as many trades as you like, individual trades can only be conducted in two currencies. What this means is that you start off with one currency and trade in another.

Common currency pairs are the US Dollar and the Euro, the Dollar and the Japanese Yen, the Euro and the Chinese Yuan, or the Dollars and the Swiss Franc. Also, the British Pound Sterling is a commonly traded currency though it isn't quite as predominant as the US Dollar. Virtually all investors speculate for or against the Dollar at any point.

For the sake of simplicity in this book, we will assume that investors are holding US Dollars and will start out trading in US Dollars. You can build up a position in any currency you feel would make a good profit for you. So, there is no restriction in that sense.

The mechanism that's used to calculate trades is known as the "exchange rate." The exchange rate is the value of one currency expressed in another. This is what you commonly see when you travel to another country. You need to exchange currency in order to purchase local currency that you can use to buy and sell. This is the pricing mechanism that FOREX uses to calculate the magnitude of a trade.

In general, the more valuable currency will translate into a greater amount of the less valuable currency. For instance, currency A is more valuable than currency B. So, the exchange rate would reflect this as 2 to 1, that is, 1 unit of currency A gets you 2 units of currency B. When there is a 1 to 1 ration, you assume that both currencies are worth the same. While this rarely happens in today's economy, it should be noted some currencies are awfully close to a 1 to 1 ratio. In such cases, there is very little room to make a profit unless you either invest a large sum or make multiple transactions that add up over time.

Fundamental Mechanics of FOREX Trading

So, let's assume that you are holding 100 US Dollars (USD). Since this is your starting point, you need to analyze which currency you wish to trade. In this case, let's consider the Euro (EUR) as it is the most commonly traded pair.

Let's assume there is a 1 to 1.10 exchange rate, meaning that 1 EUR will get you 1.10 USD. Therefore, the EUR is more valuable than the USD. When you take 100 USD and purchase EUR, you will receive 90.9 EUR. Now, to make money, you would have to speculate that the USD falls in value. Let's say the exchange rate is now 1 to 1.15. Under this assumption, the 90.9 EUR you have is now worth 104.54 USD. In this example, you stand to make a profit of 4.54 USD when you convert the EUR back into USD.

This transaction is an example of the investor betting against the USD. This is important to note because had the USD and the EUR gone to a 1 to 1 ratio, the investor would have lost 10 USD.

In addition, this example highlights how you are only flipping one currency for another and back. This can work when you are working in market conditions where there is a relative amount of volatility, that is, changes in the exchange rates. This is what can allow you to make short-term gains. When you have currency pairs that are relatively stable, you may have to hold out a bit longer to make money.

Alternatively, you could trade USD into EUR and then take those EUR and make another trade pitting another currency against the EUR. In this case, you are speculating that this particular currency would drop in value against the EUR, thereby making the EUR much more valuable against it. As you can see, these transactions can be as complex as you would like them to be.

It should also be noted that these transactions which we have described are known as the "spot" market. This means that all positions are settled in cash and are based on the 1 to 1 trade of currency. This is important to note as there are various amounts of derivatives based on currency. Derivatives are contracts in which special agreements are made involving currency. One such example is a futures contract. A futures contract is essentially a promise to buy or sell a currency at some point in the future. This is ideal for individuals and companies that may need a foreign currency at some point in the future but may not be certain of it. It helps them lock in a specific exchange rate, especially when there is a large degree of uncertainty in the global market.

How to Get Started with FOREX Trading

Virtually all trading is now conducted electronically. The days of brokers pounding the trading floor are not quite as predominant as they once were. This means that you can trade in FOREX from the comfort of your home or office. However, it isn't quite as simple as that. You need to gain access to the FOREX marketplace through a trading platform. A trading platform is a piece of software that is used to conduct trades. This platform is developed by duly licensed financial institutions. As such, you are granted access to this platform by the financial institution to trade on their behalf. In essence, this makes you a stockbroker, so to speak. The difference is that you are not paying a professional money manager a commission to handle your funds. You are doing that on your own.

To get started with a FOREX trading platform, you can do a quick online search to find the options available to you. For the purpose of this book, we will not name any specific platforms as we are not endorsing any of them, in any way, shape, or form. That's why it's up to you to conduct your own research so that you can find the one that offers you the best overall choice.

That being said, gaining access to a trading platform generally consists of purchasing a subscription. Subscriptions vary in cost and in services offered. Generally speaking, they offer access to the trading platform in addition to analytics services. These analytics, as we will discuss later on, are used to conduct technical analysis and fundamental analysis. These types of analysis help you base your decision on statistical models. This is why we have stated from the outset of this book that you need to conduct research in order to avoid basing your decisions on hunches and guesses. Please bear in mind that guessing will only lead you to subpar, if not disappointing, results.

Also, please make sure that you get all of the information regarding the cost of membership, fee per trade (or transaction), and any minimum account balance that you need to maintain. Please note that if transaction fees are high, these may end up zapping your profits. So, it's important to do your homework on potential platforms.

Reasons Why FOREX Is a Good Investment Opportunity

Unlike other types of investment opportunities such as day and swing trading, FOREX offers a greater deal of flexibility and the chance to make sizeable returns. Day trading generally consumes a lot of time in terms of research and actual trading. Day traders are subject to market hours and need to place trades at the beginning and the end of the day. Otherwise, they may leave positions open or risk losing on their deals as a result of overnight trading.

With FOREX, you don't need to invest a great deal of money. Most FOREX trading accounts have minimums of $300 to $500. While that's not chump change, it pales in comparison to the thousands of dollars that professional day traders move around on a single day. The best part of FOREX trading is that you can conduct trades for a few minutes at a time, cash out, and be certain that you know exactly where your money is.

Also, given the fact that FOREX is a 24-hour market, you can trade any time. This is perfect if you are looking to supplement your income. After all, most folks look into trading as a means of bringing in more money. Sure, it would be great to hit the jackpot and become a millionaire, but at least early on, that's not very likely. As such, looking to invest in FOREX early on as a part-time deal is a great way to find your footing.

There are plenty of folks who start out in FOREX looking to earn an extra $200 or $300 a month. From there, you can increase your expectations and perhaps bringing a couple of extra thousand dollars a month. If you put in the time and effort to become really good at it, you can even make more than your regular salary. This is what enables some folks to become full-time traders. And while they may not become uber-wealthy, they make enough to earn a decent living.

Chapter 14: Day Trading

Day trading is basically the purchasing and selling of securities within a single trading day in any marketplace at common stock markets and foreign exchange (FOREX) for the purpose of obtaining a compound of short-term loans. Day traders involved in this are fully investing in this trading activity with multiple learning sources, learning time, and good capital often end up being so successful. Being successful in day trading literally means acquiring large chunks of profits.

Characteristics of a Day Trader

Being a day trader does not come out naturally; a specific personality and traits are duly required. Below are some characteristics of a day trader:

Disciplined

This is a major trait that day traders really need to input. Day traders should always be disciplined to remain input when no opportunities emerge and really act so fast when opportunities are available. Acting fast also includes strictly considering the step by step rules and obligations initially formed in their big plans.

Open-minded

Day trading is a learning kind of income-generating engagement, implying that there are going to be happy times and downfalls. Save yourself and learn from all that. Improve the happy times and completely discard the wrong downfall moves. Being exposed to the winnings and failures makes you open-minded, a master of all possible win moves.

A fan of technology

Day trading is carried out in various trading platforms and systems that a trader needs to be familiarized with. This should not scare you. Getting to know how they work does not, in any case, require you to be a computer whiz. Get to learn the basic moves and grow technologically with time.

Mentally tough

Losing market trades are constant; most successful traders will have losing trades every single day. They typically win slightly more times than they lose. It is, therefore, essential to stay focused and rational during a losing period and do not let in the basic fact that money has been lost too. Focus on the future day trading activities by implementing some strategies outlined in a big plan.

Independence

Independence is striving to build your own toolbox that will forever lead you. Reading trading books, watching each and every video, interacting with one mentor after the other, can be a total miss. What if different books have one confusing point on a particular field? What is your YouTube subscriber who decides to quit vlogging? Always grasp the basics after in-depth research and day stay put. Dare to yourself that you've got you and get the large chunks of benefits. However, when you feel you are so lost, do not hesitate to get assistance. Most importantly, master and analyze successful moves and let them be a part of your big plan.

Patience

Good things do take quite some time. In every strategical move, you try to make, think about it carefully, but this should not make you paranoid. Act accordingly with many disciplines to reduce the number of losses likely to be incurred during various day trading activities.

Also, a patient day trader is a learning day trader. Day trading is not going to be easy at first, but with time, when you will be equipped with lots of skills and experience, things are expected to flow very smoothly. Hey, be patient.

Future-oriented

Getting stuck in the past makes you much of a prisoner. Forward-thinking lets you see the possible moves and gives you the decisive air when the next trading activity will occur considering the set protocols in the day trader's plan. Being future-oriented incites forward-thinking, which involves rational thinking and knowing your next possible moves after a considerate examination. Being future-oriented hastens and simplifies the day trading operation moves, and chances are that they are going to be successful.

Financial freedom

Day trading does not necessarily require you to be a tycoon, but you are required to have a specific amount of money that has been precisely selected to begin day trading. Remember, first times are always win or lose situations; however, as you continue to learn and grow, this set of money can be lost too. Be careful about how you handle your finances in day trading. Not every story is a good one.

Enthusiasm

High interest in something is a pending successful goal. A great enthusiastic inclination to stocks, securities, commodities, markets, and business gives you the thirst to learn and master what day trading is all about. These are signs of a future successful day trader.

Experience and familiarity

Experience comes with pretty much of downfall lessons and learning. Expose yourself to different learning sources and master every profitable move during day trading to squeeze the best out of that. Getting the actual experience and familiarity of the trading platforms and various strategies needed to be successful at day trading is worthwhile.

Difference Between Long and Short Trade

In stock markets, the terms long and short basically imply whether a trade was initiated by first selling or first purchasing. A long trade is initiated when the day trader purchases at a special price to sell at a higher price in the future in a bid to get profits. In contrast, short trades are initiated with selling, before even purchasing, to repurchase at a lower price from the market and eventually acquire profits.

Short selling is simply:

Borrow the stock.

Sell the stock.

Buyback the stock?

Profit or loss?

Risks are also involved during short selling; stock prices may end up being so high, and usually, there is no limit to how a particular price can actually go.

During long trading, your profit potential is unlimited, since the price of the asset can rise indefinitely.

Can One Do Day Trading for a Living?

The first point to take down is yes; day trading is a lucrative engagement. However, that does not mean that it is way simple than any other actual job. And yes, you get to be your own boss. You get to do it your way, on your time, with your strategies for a living. It is amazing. We do not get so lucky in this life, though; drawbacks have to appear too. Below, let us venture on the different pros and cons that come with day trading.

Benefits:

Own boss

Getting to work the way you desire has always been the best thing ever. Your plan, your moves, your strategies. This is so good, imagine going for a vacation without first passing through the Human Resource department with some great explanation so that your reason can be valid enough. Moreover, getting to work for you already gives you the full energy to make things really alive. You have enough spirit of learning and bringing out the best in you. Do yourself a huge favor and be your own boss.

Comfort.

A peaceful working environment enhances the quality of the end product, or rather, the aftermath turns out to be so successful. A peaceful environment creates a much-concentrated workspace. Day traders get to strictly master the actual day trading activities and learn more every day. This will, in the end, accomplish their big plans as indicated by the large chunks of profit that will be made.

Risk management.

Exposure to day to day cases of day trading will definitely make you a better risk-taker. Day trading is made up of so many risks that act as a day to day lesson. The trader gets to master the proper moves and discard the previously made mistakes so as to become a successful day trader.

Technologically advantaged.

Day trading exposes you to the internet as you try to get access to various sources. The internet is technology, so full of technology. You are exposed to new sites and different technological techniques. This builds you because technology is the present and the future.

Drawbacks:

A solitary lifestyle.

Day trading is a peace of mind activity, implying that physical noise should not be a part of it. This creates a lonely kind of environment since the trader is mostly by himself or herself trying to master the possible right moves. You are really going to enjoy day trading if the best company usually is just your company.

Inconsistent salary figure.

Your smart trading work will be reflected by the salary figure you obtain every single trading day. When you decide to take a day off, no gains are promised. At one particular point, you may gain like $3000, and the next day you experience $2000 loss, no consistent salary figures are promised, your smart moves are the ones that will get you a Lamborghini.

How to Decide on What and When to Buy

When and what exactly to buy in day trading is so fundamental. Let us outline some factors that have to be considered.

Understand that a level of risk is involved and the risk level suitable for you.

There is a bunch of stocks to trade with different rates of volatility, price, and volume characteristics. There are different kinds of risks experienced in each and every level of day trading. As a beginner, pick the risk level that matches your risk management rate. Day to day trading activities exposes you to several kinds of risks that frequently occur, so every trading day becomes a learning day. With time, a beginner is exposed to all types of possible risks that are likely to be educative, and he or she gets to be a pro in handling risks.

Analyze and come up with the right kinds of prices to buy.

Your personality totally describes you. Therefore, judging from it, you should favor yourself with the kind of day market you want to get involved in. For instance, if you have a fast mind, yet you can really focus despite the string of actions needed at a particular circumstance, you should go for short term trading.

Focus and analyze one specific stock.

Keep it simple. Deal with a particular stock at a time. Understand how it is handled, explore all its sides, and examine how it is operated at multiple time frames. Every stock has its own characteristics and personality meaning that you need to understand its behavior in order to anticipate the right moves.

Explore several trading charts to understand the stock movement and the overall market performances.

Charts act as a pictorial representation of the actual activities that are taking place in the day trading market. They help to monitor and express every moment taking place during trading. A beginner is obliged to master and learn every move that is depicted from the charts for future successful moves in day trading.

Be disciplined and strictly stick with your plan.

Strictly following up the initial strategical set plan is a successful move-in day trading. Being disciplined enough to follow what was examined and noted down as a step guarantees the day trader a zero chance of incurring large chunks of losses.

Chapter 15: Swing Trading and Strategies

There are numerous ways of trading financial assets or securities. One of the best strategies for retail investors is swing trading. Swing trading is a trading style or strategy where a trader enters a position and will exit this position within a period of a single trading day up to a couple of months. The average period is usually two days to about two weeks.

Swing trading is a favorite strategy for most retail traders. They love this trading style because it allows time for life. You can trade and make money while going about your daily routine. You can still go to work, take care of your family, study or play, and still make money on the side.

If you want to trade and be profitable whilst still doing everything that you like, then you should learn how to swing trade. A lot of very successful traders are swing traders. One of the best known of them is Warren Buffet. You will, therefore, be in great company. We will take a close look at swing trading and examine how it applies to options. But first, let us take a look at some of the characteristics of options.

Main Characteristics of Options

1. Underlying Asset

One of the major characteristics of options is the underlying asset. An option is always based on financial security such as a stock. It can also be based on an asset or a commodity like gold. The price of the stock is determined by the price of the underlying asset.

2. Call and Put Options

When it comes to options, we have two very basic types. These are called options and put options. All other options are premised off these two major or basic types. A call option is an options contract that awards its holder rights to the underlying security but no obligations.

3. The Strike Price

The strike price is the price at which an option holder can sell the underlying stock if he or she opts to invoke their right. This price is usually fixed and cannot be changed afterward.

4. Expiration Date

Another useful characteristic of options is the expiration date. All options must have an expiration date. Their lives are not infinity like stocks but limited. When purchasing or selling options, the expiration date features strongly.

Crucial Features of Options Contracts

There are other important features we need to learn about options. One is that options are extremely flexible. Sometimes the contracts appear to be highly standardized such they can only be transacted at certain exchanges. Here are some standout features of options contracts.

1. Very Flexible

Options contracts are, on one hand, extremely standardized such that they can only be purchased and sold at exchanges. Also, such options contracts cannot be adjusted to meet the desires of every buyer and seller. As such, they are rather standard. But certain options contracts are privately arranged. In this case, a writer will sit down and discuss certain aspects of the contract with a buyer.

2. A Down Payment

There is an upfront payment that a buyer always has to pay. This amount is known as the premium. It is the amount that the buyer has to pay to have the right to the option. Premiums are often very affordable compared to the cost of stocks or other underlying securities. For instance, the cost of premiums ranges from $1 to around $5 per 100 shares. This is much lower than the actual cost of shares or any underlying security. This amount is also a consideration for the premium writer. Writers usually make their profits from the premium amount. This is how it works out. During discussions, the premium amount has to feature.

3. Final Settlement

During the drafting of the options contract, no money changes hands. What happens is once the options contract takes effect, the buyer will take possession after payment of the premium. Settlement takes place after an options contract holder sells it or exercises their right. Remember that the options contract ceases to exist once the right is exercised or upon expiration. It is at this point that settlement of the contract takes place. In the event the option is not exercised then there is no settlement needed. The option will expire worthlessly.

4. Options are Non-Linear

Options contracts lack the properties of linearity which is evident in other securities such as stocks and bonds. What this means is that the profit earned after the underlying security's movement is not equivalent to the losses possible. This means that the underlying securities movement in one direction will not yield a profit that is equal to the loss possible

Trading options is considered by some to be a complex subject. However, it is only complex when it is compared to simpler investments such as sale and purchase of stocks or trade-in basic stocks and so on. Most traders get to understand this subject once they have a clearer picture of how options work.

Trading options is a strategy that is occasionally used by experienced traders to leverage securities and mitigate against certain risks inherent in the markets. If a trader holds certain stocks but expects the price to fall because of certain reasons, then the trader could use options to mitigate against the risks of loss.

Ordinarily, investors often buy low then sell high to be profitable. However, this is not always the case with options. When it comes to options trading, a trader can make money when the prices are low, when they are high, and even when the market moves sideways only.

Options trading can be extremely useful to investors in different ways. Traders can use options to protect their investments from losses. They can also trade directly in options and make huge and astronomical profits. However, the options trading process is an extremely risky affair. Chances of traders losing their money are high. Even the best of traders does lose some of their trades.

The risk is considered serious because traders stand to lose not just the entire investment but losses can sometimes be unlimited. This means traders can be liable for losses larger than what they bargained for. That is why it is advisable to trade cautiously and only engage in trades that are simple and less complicated. In general, the more complicated a strategy is, the riskier it is. There are other factors associated with the options trade. These include time decay and implied volatility.

The options trading process is a bit more complicated compared to selling and buying of stocks. Sometimes buying or selling options is a huge gamble. It is also much more difficult to gain approval as an options trader compared to a regular trader. Also, it is highly advisable to consider the consequences and effects of trading options especially with variables such as time decay and implied volatility.

However, much as options trading process is thought to be complex and highly risky, the fundamentals are relatively easy to follow and comprehend. And that is where it all begins. A good trader needs to develop a strong foundation and a clear understanding of a concept and then building up from there. As soon as you can understand the basics of options trading, you will then be in a position to understand more complex features and details about options.

Reasons for Trading Options

Traders may wonder why the need to diversify into options when other securities are doing just fine. The important point that needs to be understood is that options can be extremely profitable in certain instances and offer different ways of profiting. A trader can make money in any market condition. This means money can be made when the markets are bullish, bearish, or experience no movement at all.

1. Potential for Astronomical Profits

One of the main reasons for trading options is the opportunity of making significantly large profits compared to all other forms of trade in the markets. This is possible even without large sums of money. The principle behind this approach is leverage. A trader needs not to have large amounts of funds to earn huge profits. For instance, with as little as $10,000, it is possible to earn amounts such as $300,000 or even $800,000 simply by using leverage.

Take the example of a trader whose trading fund is $10,000. The trader wishes to invest this amount in Company ABC. Now the current stock price is $20 though this price is expected to rise. The trader could use the funds to purchase the shares directly and receive a total of 500 shares for his money. If the stock price was to rise to $25 within a month, the trader will have made $5 per share or a total of $2,500 in profits.

Alternatively, the trader could purchase call options of XYZ stocks with the same amount of money. The options allow the trader to purchase back the underlying stocks within a certain period. Now, options contracts cost between $1 and $4 depending on certain factors such as the value of the underlying security. In our example, one call options costs $2 so for the $10,000, the trader receives 5,000 options contracts.

If the trader chooses to exercise the right to sell the underlying shares in the following month, then he stands to make a profit of $5 per share. Remember that he has a right to a total of 5,000 shares for a total profit of $25,000. This demonstrates the capacity and power of options as well as how profitable this kind of trade can be.

2. Great Risk vs. Reward Consideration

Like all good traders, it is essential to weight the risk posed by a certain trade compared to the possible rewards. When trading using options, then the style adapted will indicate the type of risk inherent in the trade. The above example clearly shows how profitable options trading process is. If a loss were to be incurred in the above instance, then the total loss would have been the cost of the options.

In this instance, the risk is well worth the reward because the amount set to be lost is insignificant compared to the amount of profit to be made. In general, the higher the risk than the higher the potential return. Any time that a trader considers a trade, then the risk versus reward ratio should be taken into consideration.

As an options trader, you should learn how to benefit from volatility. Volatility needs to be your friend and partner as you can benefit from sharp and sudden movements in the markets. Options are mostly affected by implied volatility which is essentially the most crucial factor affecting options prices. You need to learn to be on the lookout for implied volatility and determine whether it is low or high. This way, you will easily be able to get a sense of direction regarding the type of options to engage with.

3. Versatility and Flexibility

Another extremely appealing benefit of trading in options is the inherent flexibility. Options offer lots of flexibility with dozens of different strategies to pursue. This compares well with numerous other trade and investment options out there. Most of these do not offer as much flexibility as options do. Also, most other securities have limited strategies and this tends to limit the flexibility that a trader has on that security.

Chapter 16: Calls and Puts

Now we are going to take a look at options from a different angle. Up until this point, our focus has been on buying and then trading options on the market. But there is another way to make money using options if you are somebody who owns shares of stock. And as we will discover, it turns out you don't need to actually own the shares of stock in order to make some money. Although, you will want to keep in mind that some of the possibilities we are going to examine are riskier than others.

If you recall, when you buy an option, you pay a premium for it. Now, you have good chances that when you buy an option during your regular trading, you are probably buying it from somebody who bought it from somebody else and so on. But at some point, someone sold to open the option. So, whoever purchased it, from the writer of the option, paid them the premium, which the seller could use as their own income. Selling options can be a nice way to make a good monthly income.

There are a couple of different ways that you can go about doing this. The first way is to actually own the shares of stock that you use as collateral to cover the option. Remember that there is a chance that an option might be exercised. So that possibility is always there. And if you don't own the shares of stock or have money to cover a purchase, it could be a real problem.

Certain people sell options that then they don't even own the underlying stock for, or have the financial backing to purchase shares, and these are called naked calls and naked puts.

When it comes to selling options, you have to think not only about whether it is a call option or a put, but you also have to consider whether or not it is covered or naked. Either way, the primary goal in most cases is to make income via monthly or weekly payments from selling options. Let's get started by looking at the simplest case, which is a covered call.

Covered Calls

A covered call works in the following way. The seller of the covered call owns at least 100 shares of the underlying stock. People may be speculating that the price of the stock is going to go up. But you can always take a chance if you think that the stock is not going to go up as much as somebody who is trading options is hoping it will go up. Although the price of an out of the money call is not going to be the best price that you could get for an option, the fact that it is out of the money cuts the risk that you will lose your shares if someone exercises the option. Secondly, time decay will work in your favor, since as time passes, if the option remains out of the money, it becomes worthless to the buyer. This might seem a bit confusing at first, so let me give you an example.

Suppose that there is a stock that is trading at $100 dollars a share. Consider selling a slightly out of the money call using shares that are already owned to cover it. In this case, we could choose a strike price that is a little bit higher than the market price for the stock right now. For this example, I will choose a $102 strike price with a 30-day expiration date. The price of the option is $2.57. So, if we had 100 shares, we could make $257 by selling the option. If you had 1,000 shares, you could sell 10 options contracts and make $2,570.

But remember there are risks involved in any financial transaction. In this case, the risk is actually fairly low. It is possible that the price of the stock will rise and go above $102, over a 30-day period. And it is also possible that somebody will choose to exercise their option to buy the shares if that happens. Even if they don't, if it goes in the money, the broker can still exercise the option.

Of course, most of the time, stock prices don't fluctuate all that much. But let's say that the price rose to $103. In this situation, it is possible, although certainly not guaranteed, that somebody might exercise the option. If they did so, you would have to sell your shares at $102 per share. But you can buy an option back if necessary, as a way to get out of that kind of trouble.

The stock was trading at $100 dollars per share when you wrote the option, so really you are selling the stock at a higher price, and this is not that big of a deal. You are missing out on the $1 higher price that you could have sold the stock at, had you not written the options contract.

However, you sold the option for $2.57. Then you sell the shares for $102, which is a gain of $2 per share. Now add on the $2.57 per share that you got from selling the options contract, and we are up to $4.57 in earnings per share. So, although you lose a theoretical dollar, had you sold the stock on the open market, which brings us down to $3.57, you still made a profit. Of course, we are not taking into account commissions, but overall, that won't have that much impact.

When it comes down to it, the actual risk involved is not really selling the stock. Yes, you are giving up a little bit of upside, but you are also still earning money. The real risk is getting in a situation where you are forced to sell shares of stock that you don't really want to sell.

In fact, that is how these options got their name as "calls." The old lingo was that your shares could be "called away" if somebody decided to exercise the option. That is why they are known as calls.

In addition to the risk that you might be giving up a future upside, there are other things to consider. If the stock pays dividends, there could be a risk involving the dividend. In simple words, if it is a dividend-paying stock, you have to keep track of the ex-dividend date. This is so that you don't get into a situation where somebody exercises their option to buy the shares, and you have to let go of the shares while also giving the buyer the dividend. So, you are probably going to want to look at the ex-dividend date and wait until that date has passed before selling to open against your shares.

Now, in the event that the stock price stays about the same or even declines, then you are in a situation where there is no risk at all. So, using our example if the stock dropped to $99 dollars a share, or even stayed about $100 a share, the option would end up expiring worthless. In that case, you keep the money you earned from the premium, and then you also keep the shares. So, if you are hoping to keep the shares for a long-term investment, then you are all good. You can then repeat the process and earn more premium by writing more options contracts based on the stock.

Some of the things that we can say about this strategy is that it is not the kind of trade that is going to cause you to lose your life savings. The worst thing that could happen is that you may have to sell the shares of stock and miss out on the little bit of profit that you could have made, should the price of the share boost way beyond the strike price. But you are still going to come out ahead financially even though it might not be as good as you could have come out. And you will have to figure out something else to do with the money once you have the shares called away. It is all money that can be reinvested.

Since the risk is relatively low for this type of transaction, brokerages allow level one traders to sell covered calls. For those of you who don't own 100 shares of any stock, unfortunately, that won't be an option for you. But if you do own some shares and you are willing to take some risk in losing the shares, then this could be a way to generate some monthly income.

Some people sell options that expire in as little time as a week because that can minimize the risk a little bit. The reason is that it has less time for the stock to go beyond the strike price and with only a week left on the option, the extrinsic for time value is decaying rapidly.

There are some other possibilities. You can do what is called a close-out. This means that you purchase the call options back, and as a result, your position is closed out. In this case, you might gain or lose money, depending on what the price of the option is at the time you buy it back. But doing this will allow you to retain your ownership of the stock. If the option is still out of the money, it will be much cheaper than you sold it for, so this won't eat into your profits very much.

There is also the possibility of doing what is called a rollout. So, what you do in this case is you buy back the covered calls and then you sell new ones that have the same strike price, but a longer expiration date. So, if you sold covered calls that expired on May 31st, when getting a rollout, you would buy them back before they expire and then sell new ones with the same strike price that expired for example on June 30th.

Roll out and up means that you do the rollout strategy, but instead of keeping the strike price the same, you sell the new options with a higher strike price. Conversely, roll out and down is when you use the rollout strategy, but you sell with a lower strike price.

For people who are not too risk-averse, there is also another possibility that of selling call options with a strike price which is actually below the trading share price. Now, why would you want to take that risk? Because the options sell for a much higher price.

Chapter 17: Options Trading and the Individual Investor

This chapter looks at the setups for profitable trades - to get a rough overview and to see where the market is in general development. Then we turn to the technical tools to find an entry point, stop-fall protection, if you're wrong, and the likely candidates for the price moves. As in the real estate business, trading is the most important factor: the location, the location, the location. Then there is the timing, the timing, the timing. The setup gives you a rough overview of the market's current state of development - key information when looking for short-term reversal or confirmation patterns. Ideally, you open your position in the area where the likelihood of success is greatest.

How Does the Stock Market Work?

A Stock market analysis definitely looks like gibberish to beginners and average investors. However, you should know that the way this market works is actually quite simple. Just imagine a typical auction house or an online auction website. This market works in the same way - it allows buyers and sellers to negotiate prices and carry out successful trades. The first stock market took place in a physical marketplace, however, these days, trades happen electronically via the internet and online stockbrokers. From the comfort of your homes, you can easily bid and negotiate for the prices of stocks with online stockbrokers.

Furthermore, you might come across news headlines that say the stock market has crashed or gone up. Once again, don't fret or get all excited when you come across such news. Most often than not, this means a stock market index has gone up or down. In other words, the stocks in a market index have gone down. Before we proceed, let's explore the meaning of market indexes.

Stock Market Indexes

As mentioned earlier, when people refer to the rise and fall of the stock market, they are generally referring to one of the major stock market's market indexes. Market indexes track the performance of a group of stocks in a particular sector like manufacturing or technology. The value of the stocks featured in an index is representative of all the stocks in that sector. It is very important to take note of what stocks each market index represents. As mentioned in the first chapter, you should invest in a niche you are comfortable with. In addition to this, giant market indexes like the Dow Jones Industrial Average, the NASDAQ composite, and the Standard & Poor's 500, are often used as proxies for the performance of the stock market as a whole. You can choose to invest in an entire index through the exchange-traded funds and index funds, as it can track a specific sector or index of the stock market.

Talking about the bullish outlook of the stock market is guaranteed to get beginners looking astonished. Yes, it sounds ridiculous at first, but with time, you get to appreciate the ingenuity of these descriptions. Let's start with the bearish market. A bear is an animal you would never want to meet on a hike; it strikes fear into your heart, and that's the effect you will get from a bearish market. A bear market depicts when stock prices are falling across several of the indexes mentioned earlier. The threshold for a bearish market varies within a 20 percent loss or more.

Most young investors unfamiliar with a bear market as we've been in a bull market since the first quarter of 2019. In fact, this makes it the second-longest bull market in history. Just as you have probably guessed by now, a bull market indicates that stock prices are rising. You should know that the market is continually changing from bull to bear and vice versa. From the Great Recession to the global market crash, these changing market prices indicate the start of larger economic patterns. For instance, a bull market shows that investors are investing heavily and that the economy is doing extremely well. On the other hand, a bear market shows investors are scared and pulling back, with the economy on the brink of collapsing. If this made you paranoid about the next bear market, don't fret. Business analysts have shown that the average bull market generally outlasts the average bear market by a large margin. This is why you can grow your money in stocks over an extended period of time.

Stock Market Corrections and Crash

A stock market crash is every investor's nightmare. It is usually extremely difficult to watch stocks that you've spent so many years accumulating diminish before your very eyes. Yes, this is how volatile the stock market is. Stock market crashes usually include a very sudden and sharp drop in stock prices, and it might herald the beginning of a bear market. On the other hand, stock market corrections occur when the market drops by 10 percent - this is just the market's way of balancing itself. The current bull market has gone through 5 market corrections.

Analyzing the Stock Market

You are not psychic. It is nearly impossible to accurately predict the outcome of your stock to the last detail. However, you can become near perfect at reading the stock market by learning how to analyze the components of this market properly. There are two basic types of analyses: technical analysis and fundamental analysis.

Fundamental Market Analysis

Fundamental analysis involves getting data about a company's stocks or a particular sector in the stock market, via financial records, company assets, economic reports, and market share. Analysts and investors can conduct fundamental analysis via the metrics on a corporation's financial statement. These metrics include cash flow statements, balance sheet statements, footnotes, and income statements. Most times, you can get a company's financial statement through a 10-k report in the database. In addition to this, the SEC's EDGAR is a good place to get the financial statement of the company you are interested in. With the financial statement, you can deduce the revenues, expenses, and profits a company has made.

What's more? By looking at the financial statement, you will have a measure of a company's growth trajectory, leverage, liquidity, and solvency. Analysts utilize different ratios to make an accurate prediction about stocks. For example, the quick ratio and current ratio are useful in determining if a company will be able to pay its short-term liabilities with the current asset. If the current ratio is less than 1, the company is in poor financial health and may not be able to recover from its short-term debt. Here's another example: a stock analyst can use the debt ratio to measure the current level of debt taken on by the company. If the debt ratio is above 1, it means the company has more debt than assets and it's only a matter of time before it goes under.

Technical Market Analysis

This is the second part of stock market analysis and it revolves around studying past market actions to predict the stock price direction. Technical analysts put more focus on the price and volume of shares. Additionally, they analyze the market as a whole and study the supply and demand factors that dictate market movement. In technical analyses, charts are of inestimable value. Charts are a vital tool as they show the graphical representation of a stock's trend within a set time frame. What's more? Technical investors are able to identify and mark certain areas as resistance or support levels on a chart. The resistance level is a previous high stock price before the current price. On the other hand, support levels are represented by a previous low before the current stock price. Therefore, a break below the support levels marks the beginning of a bearish trend. Alternatively, a break above the resistance level marks the beginning of a bullish market trend. Technical analysis is only effective when the rise and fall of stock prices are influenced by supply and demand forces. However, technical analysis is mostly rendered ineffective in the face of outside forces that affect stock prices such as stock splits, dividend announcements, scandals, changes in management, mergers, and so on. Investors can make use of both types of analyses to get an accurate prediction of their stock values.

Why You Need to Diversify

According to research by Ned Davis, a bear market occurs every 3.5 years and has an average lifespan of 15 months. One thing is clear, though: you can't avoid bear markets. You can, however, avoid the risks that come with investing in a single investment portfolio. Let's look at a common mistake that new investors typically make. Research points to the fact that individual stocks dwindle to a loss of 100 percent. By throwing in your lot with one company, you are exposing yourself to many setbacks. For example, you can lose your money if a corporation is embroiled in a scandal, poor leadership, and regulatory issues. So, how can you balance out your losses? By investing in the aforementioned index fund or ETF fund, as these indexes hold many different stocks, as by doing this, you've automatically diversified your investment. Here's a nugget to cherish: put 90 percent of your investment funds in an index fund, and put the remaining 10 percent in an individual stock that you trust.

When to Sell Your Stocks

One thing is sure - you are not going to hold your stocks forever. All our investment advice and energies are directed towards buying. Yes, it is the buying of stocks that kick-start the whole investment when chasing your dream concept. However, just as every beginning has an end, you will eventually sell every stock you buy. It is the natural order. Even so, selling off stock is not an easy decision. Heck! It's even harder to determine the right time to sell. This is the point where greed and human emotions start to battle with pragmatism. Many investors try to make sensible selling decisions solely based on price movements. However, this is not a sure strategy, as it is still sensible to hold onto a stock that has fallen in value. Conversely, selling a stock when it has reached your target is seen as prudent. So, how can you navigate around this dilemma? Before touching on other parts in this section, let's first tackle the reason why selling is so hard.

Why Selling Is So Hard

Do you know why it's so hard to let go of your stocks even when you have a fixed strategy to follow? The answer lies in human greed. When making decisions, it's an innate human tendency to be greedy. Here's an example: An investor purchases shares at $30, and tells herself that when the stocks hit $40, she will sell. Here comes an all-too-familiar trend - when the stocks finally hit $40, the investor will hold out and see if her stock prices will rise beyond $40. You can see that human nature is already creeping in. Surely, the stocks hit $45, and greed takes over logical thinking. She decides to wait to see if it rises beyond $45.

Suddenly, the stock prices plummet down to $36. At this point, she tells herself that once the stocks rise again to $40, she will sell. Unfortunately, this never happens. This stock continues to plummet down to $25. Finally, she succumbs to her frustrations and sells at $25.

Chapter 18: Candlestick Charts and Patterns

Candlestick charts weren't known in the West before the 1980s when they were introduced. However, Japan used this method for centuries, which at the same time makes Japan the place of origin of the candlestick method. As we already have seen before, these charts show the same information as the bar chart that was used in our country's way before we started using the Japanese system. The reason that the candlestick charts became so popular in such a short amount of time is the fact that it is easier to understand and it uses simple yet innovative body illustration that helps the investor seeing every change at a glance.

Let's recap some of the basic characteristics of the candlestick as the general pattern. Firstly, the total length of the candle represents the trading range for the predetermined period. The body of the candle is connected to the distance between the prices known as the closing price and the opening price. The difference in color shows if the price went up or down for a certain period. The length of the candle also portrays the volatility of the price and the sum of the candle and the "body" of the candle can be viewed as the progress that was made for one day. If the chart shows that the candle's "body" is short, it means that the closing and the opening prices were close or similar. If that is the case, we can say that the buyers and the sellers were in balance.

Types

When it comes to the candlestick chart, we can say that there are regular candles and then that there is Doji. Doji is a special candle which body is just a horizontal line. This line represents closing prices and opening prices, which in case you have Doji are equivalent.

If the candles have long bodies that will indicate that the trend of the price is strong. If your chart has candles without any wicks, it means that you got Marubozu. Marumboza is an indicator that shows that the trades were only made in the range of the opening and closing prices, thus no trade was done outside of that range. This is a very strong indication, which means that the market was strongly pushing the price only in one direction.

Hammer

When it comes to ideal signals, in Hammer that signal is represented with a small body. Its wick should be two times longer than the body regardless of the day being up or down for the price trend. Hammer sometimes signals that the trend of the price will reverse. The way to confirm such an assumption and make it actionable is to wait for the following day and see if the price is going to increase. If the price starts raising it means that your interpretation of trend reversal has been confirmed. This pattern works because many traders panic, and if the price is down for some time they would sell at any price. If we try to express this situation in the candle chart it means that the wick is going to be pushed down. However, smart investors come in and they buy which pushes the price up once again. These trend reversals can last through the whole day and even keep up happening the following day too.

Hanging Man

The Hanging Man is a pattern that looks the same as the Hammer; the only difference is that it comes in an uptrend. Just like before, we search for a change in the price trend on the following day so we could confirm our estimation of the trend's reversal. The psychology, in this case, is that traders mostly decide to take profits. That way they push the prices down. Still, some of those who are new on the market see this as their chance to buy. That way they push the price back up in any case, this candle is considered to be weak. As a reflection of this pattern, it appears that traders have a hunch that this means that the trend is over so the selling starts to rise again in the following few days.

Inverted Hammer

Once you see the diagrams for the first two candlestick patterns you will realize that the inverted hammer also has similar characteristics. There is also certain psychology behind it signaling and we will briefly explain it: Once the downtrend starts weakening and several traders have second thoughts, they start buying in which pushes the prices up. Sellers also come back in the game which means that the price will close down. However, if the price starts increasing during the following day than the conclusion is that the weakness of the trend made buyers buying even more while pushing up the prices, and that way the uptrend started.

Shooting Star

The last but not the least in the set of four related candle signals is the pattern known as the Shooting Star comes which comes in an uptrend. Everybody knows that beginners or novices if you prefer, tend to buy on the top. Shooting star demonstrates simply the exuberance that the future causes the traders to see the high wick that appears when novices enter the market. The traders who notice this are usually those who appeared thinking that it is time to sell. Just like in every other pattern above, the only way to confirm this is to wait up the following day and to determine if that was the signal that shows that the trend will reverse.

Bullish Engulfing

This is a pattern that consists of two candles and it is graded as highly probable. When in a downtrend, the first candle pressures that the selling continues. The pressure is strong enough to allow the following candle to open up at an even lower price. But those investors who are smart see an opportunity here and they start buying on the second candle in this case. This makes the price to grow and launches it above the limit of the preceding period. This is one of the numerous proofs that the real power is in the hands of the buyers and that there is a high possibility that the trend will reverse.

Bearish Engulfing

It has the same concept as bullish engulfing. The thing is that sometimes uptrend can stretch so badly that the opening price can even go higher than the current price in the earlier candle. Smart and experienced investors usually decide to sell on these occasions. The length of the candle, in this case, shows that the trend can be reversed from an uptrend to a downtrend due to the weight of an opinion.

Piercing Candle is a pattern that represents a strong bearish candle that is in a downtrend. This candle with another, following candle, opens up at a price that is lower than the current one. However, the candle is rallying to have the finishing price, which has the same trading range as the earlier day. This pattern can be seen as a signal for the trend reversal and the reason for that is piercing candle as an indicator that sellers are feeling hopeless. When the low prices go even lower it is an opportunity for those who consider themselves to be smart investors to start buying and to push prices strongly up.

Dark Cloud Cover is a pattern that has entirely the same characteristic as the piercing candle pattern. The only difference is that the dark cloud cover is in an uptrend.

Bullish Harami

This pattern has a name that originated from the Japanese word Harami that means "pregnant". As the name suggests, the reason for this is that according to them these candlestick patterns have a resemblance to the pregnant women. If you happen to encounter the bullish harami it means that the market had a lot of active sellers. However, the other candle indicates that the current price became higher. If the second candle finishes up and provides buying enough pressure, you can see it as a signal that there is going to be a change in the price trend. As usual, the following day is a confirmation checker.

Bearish Harami

When a pattern reaches an end of an uptrend there can be a candle that demonstrates exuberance that some might see as naïve. When the other period opens up and the price is lower continuing to go lower as the day goes by, we can say that it indicates second thoughts in buyers. The most probable income of this situation is that the selling will continue regularly and that everything will be resolved once when the price goes into a downtrend.

Candlestick pattern rules

Candlestick patterns named aren't the only one that exists. However, these are the main or the most popular ones that you might find useful during your trading career. Like we mentioned once before, nowadays numerous programs and servers can calculate, estimate, and identify any pattern that you are interested in. Keep in mind that trading should never be done based on one strategy or just one resource, which is why we wouldn't recommend that you start trading relying only on the information you gather through the candlestick principle for example. Remember, the validity of the pattern depends on the right trend in which the pattern needs to work in. Also, many other indicators have to be taken into consideration.

Trading Platforms

Options trading platforms come in several varieties. These are offered by brokerage firms to help you trade at any level you want. Some platforms only feature basic components while others contain more advanced features such as trade and market analytics as well as pricing tools. These are available as web-based applications or as standalone programs. The decision to use any of these lies with the investor.

Choosing the right options trading platform that suits your needs is very important because it can make your trading experience more productive and less time-consuming. However, with the wide array of platforms available on the market, selecting one that is good can become a tedious exercise. This is because some platforms are more advertised than others.

Price per trade – this is always the first consideration that investors make when they need to choose a trading platform. The price per trade refers to the amount of cash you will pay for each transaction that you complete on the platform. If you are an active trader, then you will realize how important this is each time you have to part with some fees and commissions. You must check out platforms that charge less for each trade you complete.

Monthly fees – some platforms charge investors a monthly service fee. This is always in the form of inactivity and maintenance fees. You need a platform that charges zero monthly maintenance fees as this will ensure that your investment returns remain at a maximum.

Faster execution of – this is another priority for investors and traders. If you need an account that completes your trades faster, then you must choose a platform that allows you to do this with ease. This is quite important when the options you want to trade in represent fast-moving assets. In this case, the difference between getting a profit and losing your investment lies in how fast your orders are processed. Therefore, the execution speed of transactions should be a top priority for you if you want to succeed in your trades.

Chapter 19: General Possibilities of Solving Beginners Errors

Many options for beginners start with creating sophisticated positioning strategies, such as iron condor spreads or butterfly spreads, as their first few options. Then they go utterly wrong because they didn't know how to hold a position, and some don't even know how to set areas correctly. If you're new to trading options, stick to a few simple calls or puts on topics with small amounts (or money you can afford to lose) to get an idea of how it works first before moving on to more sophisticated strategies. Complex strategies are only useful if your trading experience is as extensive as it is.

Purchasing options that don't fit your expected trading horizon

Most newbies that start trading have no idea what the expected trading horizon is and often find that the choices they buy expire before the underlying shares make the expected move. If you expect stock performance in the medium to long term, buy options that are half a year to a year off. If you do not know how the shares should behave, give yourself enough time to buy options that expire at least three months.

Delivery of incorrect orders

Under pressure, especially when it comes to real money, beginners tend to make stupid human mistakes, such as clicking the wrong button, buying the wrong option, buying the wrong expiration date, or placing the wrong stop order - a loss that position sold immediately. Such social event failures can only be mitigated by a more extended period of virtual trading practices on the institutional platform of your choice. And then gradually practice spending very little money to get used to the feeling of trading for real money. Unfortunately, we are all human beings, while experienced traders tend to make such mistakes less, but sometimes they still do. However, it is more common in ordinary trades and certainly damages trading confidence. Before opting for real money, always have a few months of virtual trading practice on the chosen platform.

Trading in borrowed money (or money you can't afford to lose)

It says, "you can't afford to win if you can't afford to lose." This is exceptional in trading, not only in options trading but in any form of trading. If you are dealing with spending money that you cannot afford to lose, mental pressure will reduce your chances of winning if your chances as a beginner are already meager. That's why we always advise people to trade only with money that they can afford to lose.

Unaccompanied trading

Do you want to learn to drive a car without being accompanied? Why would you learn to trade without being guided? Yes, a mentor or teacher is essential for beginners, not because they can give you "tips," but because they can shed light on your situation and reveal weaknesses you may not have noticed. Starting unaccompanied trading usually repeats errors over and over, and if you've traded options before, you know that clearing your account doesn't require many of these errors.

So here are the first six mistakes a beginner makes when trading stock options. Be aware of these common mistakes and avoid unnecessary frustration from losing money.

Keys to Trading Stock Options

Stock options trading gives a talented trader more potential to trade stock options than in almost any other form of online trading on the market today. The level of controlled risk associated with excellent leverage allows an experienced options trader to make huge profits. Still, an aspiring options trader should have a solid foundation in training on what a healthy option is with trading options to ensure long-term success. When developing a winning stock options system, every trader should be able to understand five essential keys.

You must first understand how much time the premium for the option you are considering trading affects. There are two parts to calculating the time when deciding on stock options. The first thing to keep in mind is your own time remaining for the option. Since options have a limited period of 30 days to several years, depending on the specific options purchased, make sure you are buying the right choice with enough time to ensure that the time does not erode your investment before your position has enough time to be profitable.

Another profit trading option is to recognize the time in your trading system about trading a particular stock option and to know the statistics of your options trading method or choice by knowing the average holding time of the trading signal. If your average option retention period is seven days, do not buy an option with a three-month premium, as you would pay more for the extra time for the purchase price of the option. Also, you would not buy an option with less than 30 days until the expiration date. As the passage of time would damage the value of the option so quickly that even if the basic movement of stock options moves positively to you, the deadline will prevent you from earning a chance to exercise.

The third thing for profitable options trading is to understand the relationship between market volatility, the underlying shares on which the option is based, and its effect on the value of the option itself. When the general stock market as an index goes through periods of volatility or low trading intervals, the stocks that make up the market tend to follow a general trend.

Also, begin to experience periods of low overall volatility, which in turn can lead to derivatives like stock options to earn cheap or level premiums. However, if market volatility increases, it is likely that individual stocks will follow the upward trend in stock options if the market shifts in favor of the trader.

Another key to successful stock options trading is to have a stock option methodology that takes these key factors into account and provides precise inputs, clear outputs, management of a defined trading system. And a profit factor more significant than your average loss in several trades. If you do not have a business methodology that would guide you through every step of the business process, you know the benefits and differences of different trading settings. A reliable trading approach keeps you on hand and defines every step because you are guided to be a consistent winner and profitable trader in the markets when everything is said and done.

Finally, the fifth and final key to successful stock trading is yourself, especially your trading psychology. People and mental makeup are incredibly complex, so stock options traders must have not only a solid method of trading stock options but also the discipline to follow their trading strategies. You can give two people the same winning trading system, but it is ubiquitous for them to have different results.

You're inevitably the one who can stay so far away from both his losing trades and his winning trades, while maintaining the discipline to follow the rules of the system, regardless of whether the trading result will ultimately be the biggest winner.

Using these five keys as a basis for developing a stock selection methodology will help you avoid the mistakes and pitfalls of many beginner options traders.

In this case, this "consistent approach" to options trading can also be referred to as a "trading system" or "options trading system." The term "trading system" is not necessarily limited to the number of automated "black box" trading signals. The trading system can be something as simple as "buying an option on an action with a raise that breaks the height of the previous lane after at least two days of withdrawal, resulting in lower low targets." A trading system is simply an organized approach that uses a repetitive pattern or event that produces a net profit.

Because an option is a "derivative" of a stock, you must derive the options trading system from the stock trading system. This means that your trading system must be based on real stock price movements. This means that your trading system may not work for all stocks; it must only work for certain types of stocks, inevitable stock volatility, and guaranteed price levels on shares, etc. Then your trading system focuses on individual stocks with price behavior that is predictable for the results you want to get from the actions.

You can develop a trading system, trading strategy, and trading methodology by identifying a price movement pattern (or missing price movement pattern) or an event that occurs regularly. This means that you can trade price behavior patterns on price charts, such as traditional chart patterns, trends, fluctuations, turning points, fields, etc.

You can trade events that motivate stock quotes, such as winning runs, after winning races, stock distribution, seasonal factors, etc. To achieve maximum profit in options trading, you want your stocks to move quickly in your favor, and you want them to go far. Only a relatively small stock price movement can double your money in options!

There are so many different strategies and combinations that you can trade options. You can buy calls and set up indicative transactions. You can use the call range and set the margin for trading in directional movements with damped risk and excess. You can sell or buy spreads and get credit for premiums payable after the option expires. If you're expecting a big step, you can trade in twigs and livestock, but you're not sure which way.

Develop a system for trading options that trade in price fluctuations. Today, there are many sound swing trading systems. We recommend that you buy it. The bottom line is that you want to swing the business with the trend. Option brokers today have advanced ordering technology that allows you to enter swing trades based on stock price movements, so you don't have to keep track of those stocks all day. Significant development to change trading opportunities.

Swing business day bars. Most trading swing systems are based on the daily pillars of a stock price chart.

Swing Intra Day Bars! Their other amazing systems are based on intraday charts linking swing records to trading.

Develop an options trading system with trends ranging from three to six months. There's a lot of money here. Dealing with significant trends is how many of them can invest more copious amounts of money in developing their net worth.

Develop a system of options related to turning points. Pivot point trading is perhaps the best way to trade options because the price action is usually explosive, and in our direction, it happens quickly when the trade works. This is great because you can use the settings in less time and make better use of them. And it's also nice that, on average, you can make big profits in five days to four weeks, which puts fewer time problems.

There are different directional trading methods that you can use to trade options. You must select, process, and never use more than 10% of the positions per second.

Small Account Trading of 1 to 5% of the maximum position size for larger accounts is a systematic approach to options money management, which is the fastest way to expand your account, avoiding unnecessary barriers quickly.

Chapter 20: Options Greeks

Now that we know what influences the prices of options, we are going to make that more quantifiable. This is done using the so-called "Greeks," which are five parameters denoted by Greek symbols (or letters) that quantify the way the price of an option will change. You don't have to know how they work precisely, only what they mean. At any given time, you can look them up to get their values. We start by looking at intrinsic value, that is, how the price of the option changes or varies with the underlying stock's price.

Delta

If you look at the data for any option, you are going to see five Greek letters (usually expressed by their English spelled names) delta, theta, gamma, vega, and rho. The first of these is delta, which tells you how the price of an option changes with the price of the underlying stock.

We noted earlier that the price of an option doesn't have a 1-1 change in price in relation to the stock. You can see exactly how it will change by looking at delta. First, we'll consider call options. So, if delta is 0.46, that means if the underlying stock price rises by $1, the price of the option is going to increase by $0.46. If delta were 0.74, then the price of the option would rise by $0.74 if the price of the underlying stock went up by $1.

Put options have a negative delta, which just indicates that a put option has an inverse relationship to the price of the underlying stock. That is if the price of the underlying stock goes down, the value of a put option goes up, and if the price of the underlying stock goes up, the value of the put option goes down.

So, if delta is -0.26, and the price of the underlying stock went up by $1, the value of the put option would drop by 26 cents. On the other hand, if the price of the underlying stock had dropped by $1, then the price of the put option would rise by $0.26.

Delta is dynamic, and the number always changes when some important parameter in the options price changes. Consider an option on a stock that is trading at $102 with a strike price of $100, with 14 days to option expiration. In this case, the price of the call option is $2.48, and delta is 0.75. The price of the put option is $0.47, and delta for the put option is -0.25. So, if the price of the underlying stock goes up by $1, we expect the call option to rise to $2.48 + $0.75 = $3.23. The price of the put option would decrease to $0.47 - $0.25 = $0.22.

That's just about what happens, but in reality, the relationship isn't quite exact since other things impact the price of the options. The call option increases to $3.84, and the put option declines in price to $0.27.

We said its dynamic, and what happens when the share price rises by $1, is the delta values for both options change as well. Now delta is 0.84 for the call, and -0.16 for the put.

That tells us something important, namely that delta is higher the more in the money the stock is. We can see this looking at some real options. Considering an IBM $124 call that expires on 6/28, it has a delta of 0.967. A $139 call that expires on 6/28 has a delta of 0.5388. The share price is $139.20, so the $124 call is more in the money. The $139 call is practically at the money, and we learn a second important fact about delta, that is that at the money options will have a delta that is reasonably close to 0.50.

Since the more in the money you are, the higher delta, that means in the money options can benefit (or be hurt by) a $1 change in the price of the underlying stock.

Something else that happens is that if the option is in the money, the closer you get to expiration, the higher delta goes. For our example of an option with a $100 share price, if the underlying stock price remains at $103, moving to 7 days from expiration, delta jumps to 0.92 for the call. Moving to 3 days to expiration, delta is 0.98. So, if you are expecting a stock price to move a lot in the next few days, getting an option that will expire soon before the move happens could be a worthwhile investment. Look for events that could impact the price, such as earnings call or product announcement.

Remember at the money options have a delta of about 0.50, and when you get close to expiration, delta for a call will be exactly 0.50, and for a put, it will be -0.5, if the option was at the money. Actually, buying at the money options can be quite difficult, so you'll probably have to settle for something close.

If an option is out of the money, the closer to the expiration date, you get the smaller delta gets. In fact, a few days away from expiration delta can get vanishingly small. An out of the money call option for a strike price of $100, share price of $97 with three days to expiration will have a delta of 0.02.

The delta for the same put option will add up the difference to 100 (but remember it's expressed as a negative value). In this case, a put option with the same parameters, so a strike price of $100 – will have a delta of -0.98 if the underlying price is $97. In that case, the put would be worth $3.00, and if the underlying share price dropped to $96, the price of the put would rise to $4. Then you'd see delta increase to -1.00 for the put and drop to 0.00 for the call.

If the stock had moved the other way, risen in price by $1, then delta for the put would drop to -0.92 instead, and the price of the put would drop to $2.04.

The bottom line is delta will give you a good estimate of how much the price of the option will change when the price of the underlying stock changes by $1. If it's a call option, the relationship is direct, and delta is expressed as a positive number. For put options, since the relationship is an inverse one, delta is a negative number. And remember that if you take the absolute value of delta for the put option and add it to the delta value for a call option that has the same strike value and date of expiration, they will sum to 1.0.

Gamma

Gamma is like the second derivative. In other words, it tells you how delta itself changes. This is important since we noted that delta was dynamic. However, beginning traders don't need to dive into this too deeply, but you can check gamma to see about how much delta will change if there is a $1 change in the price of the underlying shares. Gamma has the same value for both puts and calls. So if Gamma were 0.22 and delta was 0.24 for a call option, and -0.76 for a put option with the same strike and expiration date, we'd expect a $1 rise in share price to cause delta for the call option to increase to 0.46, and the delta for the put option would change to -0.54. That is about what would happen, but remember if the option were at the money the values of delta would move to 0.5 and -0.5, respectively.

Theta

When examining options, theta is a very important parameter among the Greeks. What theta gives you information about is the time decay of the option. Theta is expressed as a negative number, reflecting the fact that time decay causes a decrease in option price as time goes on. Let's consider a couple of examples.

Suppose that we have call and put options with a strike price of $100 with three days to expiration. The price of the call is $1.20, and the price of the put is $0.20 if the share price of the underlying stock is $101. In this case, theta is -0.073 for both the call and the put. That tells us that if nothing else changes, the price of each option will decrease by $0.073. The call option is priced at $1.20, and the put is priced at $0.20. Moving to 2 days to expiration and leaving everything else the same, we find that the price of the call option drops to $1.12, and the price of the put option drops to $0.12, so it moved in almost exact accordance to what was expected. The following day theta has increased to -0.079, reflecting the fact that time decay happens more rapidly the closer you get to the expiration date of the option.

In fact, with everything else unchanged, 20 days to expiration theta is about half as strong, at -0.035. That reflects one of the fundamental truths of options, that is that time decay happens in an exponential fashion, with time decay happening faster the closer you get to expiration.

One of the things that help make options seem complicated is that all of these variables are interdependent. So, at 20 days to expiration, suppose the stock price shot up to $108. In that case, theta decreases to -0.005. So, it's only 1/7th of the previous value. It decreases for the put option as well.

Theta is also proportional to share price. So, theta is larger if the share price is larger. Consider a stock with a share price of $975, and a strike price of $1,000. In that case, theta is -0.282 for the call option and -0.274 for the put option. That means if a day passes and nothing else changes, the value of the call option (which in this case is $5.15) will drop by about $0.28, and the value of the put option will drop by about $0.27.

The fundamental lesson here is the same as it was previously, that time decay is an important fundamental when it comes to options pricing. Check the Greek theta to get an idea of how the price of the option is going to decay by the following day if all other things are held equal.

Chapter 21: The Best Five Option Trading Strategies

Even though options trading is regularly viewed as hazardous (and it surely can be), it is common both more secure and substantially more beneficial than stock trading. The remarkable thing about options trading is that it considers a tremendous assortment of methodologies to be built up that all have different danger profiles. Even though broker expenses for options trading are fundamentally higher than those for practically some other sort of trading, this is effectively counterbalanced by the immense gainfulness accessible.

The reason that options trading has pulled in the notoriety of being excessively dangerous is that numerous traders, driven by pure greed, have attempted to accomplish most extreme returns in the base time. Madly enormous benefits are certainly conceivable; however, when dealt with a greed motive, crash-and-consumes are unavoidable. The way to fruitful alternative trading is to "claim" a strategy, to know it personally, and to utilize it reliably and with obviously characterized trading rules.

These are (as I would like to think) the perfect options trading techniques that limit hazard and give excellent benefits:

Selling Credit Spreads - with no work, and around 30 minutes per week, it is conceivable to develop your portfolio by 10-15% consistently. Achievement relies upon straightforwardness, and this is certainly not a strategy appropriate for hyperactive traders or the individuals who love to over break down everything. You should know how to do a straightforward pattern investigation on the market and your gathering of painstakingly chosen stocks. This strategy is entirely productive and is more straightforward than tumbling off a bull at a rodeo (and significantly less excruciating).

You are selling Naked Puts. This procedure works in an upward floating business sector and has a to some degree higher edge need than that of credit spreads. You can get practically identical returns, and the peril profile is comparably as low. Strangely, like credit spreads, you get your advantage ahead of time.

You are buying and selling DITM (Deep-in-the-money) options. This is a great swing trading strategy and empowers you to successfully purchase stocks at about discounted, thus twofold your benefit. Since your trades are for the most part short term (3-10 days), you are not worried about profits or different elements identifying with buying and holding stocks. However, you do benefit because the value development of the stock coordinates the value development of the choice that you acquired.

Selling Covered Calls - if you possess a stock, you can viably decrease the expense of that stock by selling secured approaches that stock each month. This is a strategy that stock traders ought not to be managing without, yet don't utilize it if you claim to stock for sentimental reasons - stock trading must be your business. Along these lines, if you infrequently get got out and end up selling your inventory, you can rapidly proceed onward to the following one.

Sophisticated methodologies, similar to straddles, chokes, iron condors, and butterflies. These are on the whole generally safe, very beneficial methodologies. Their solitary weaknesses are that they are for the most part costly (either costly options or higher broker charges due to the number of trades included).

Utilizing Option Trading Strategies as Your Core Trading Vehicle

Choice trading can be dangerous yet can likewise be progressively protected and gainful contrasted with stock trading. Choice trading procedures can be made in an assortment of ways so the hazard factor will differ and enable you to settle on increasingly beneficial choices in your trading. With this broadening, utilizing alternative trading techniques as your center trading vehicle can be more secure and significantly more gainful than trading stocks carefully. This section will clarify which kind of options to use as the critical strategy in your trading portfolio.

Presently with regards to options, the procedures are constant. You could trade calls and puts, exposed options, secured calls, spreads, etc. Numerous traders utilize a few, all or a couple of these techniques — contingent upon what you need to achieve in your portfolio, there no wrong strategy. Nonetheless, choice spreads can make a great strategy, which can convey safe benefits on a month to month premise.

Here is a rundown of alternative spreads to use in your portfolio.

Put or Call (Debit) Spreads - Works well when you know the bearing of the stock. Since you are buying this spread, you need the stock unpredictability to below to get the modest choice costs.

Iron Condors (Sell) - This sort of spread will, as a rule, be the foundation of the alternative strategy. At the point when the stock market unpredictability is steady, this strategy can be genuinely beneficial. The drawback is it doesn't function admirably in unstable markets or on reasonable options.

Vertical (Credit) Spreads - one leg of the iron condor. Use amid moderate unpredictability.

Timetable (Debit) Spreads - Since you are buying, use amid low unpredictability.

Corner to corner (Credit) Spreads - Great for gentle long-term patterns.

Be that as it may, as is in all options these options due have hazard also and you ought to counsel with your broker and paper trade until you have an exhaustive comprehension. The other pleasant part about these spread options is you need knowledge of essential pattern examination of the market and on your chose stocks.

Step by step instructions to Profit with Options Trading Strategies

Stock options trading has been accessible for right around 40 years. Traders have built up a comprehension of options trading which have delivered options trading methodologies.

This may seem like rambling nonsensically however consider it. Without the capacity to trade in a specific security, there can be no techniques. It is systems that produce benefits and as a matter of course, misfortunes.

This part does not discuss misfortunes as the creator trusts misfortunes represent themselves. Then again, benefits can be slippery and must be monitored intensely. Henceforth this specific benefit guarding strategy.

It happens very frequently a trader is in a generally unusual benefit position; however, neglects it because of mindlessness or conviction it will go higher or some other basis. This strategy will keep that from occurring.

This strategy is likewise material to online options trading. A benefit is a benefit regardless of where created. In the options world, an interest can occur in merely minutes, so it is ideal to ensure it.

Stock traders have been utilizing this strategy for quite a long time. It has satisfied abundantly.

You put a trailing stop-misfortune on the necessary security. Traders utilize various rates for their stop-misfortune point. Presumably, the most widely recognized number is 5% because it keeps a high level of the benefit unblemished. Anything higher could radically cut into the hard-earned gain.

Math astute it would appear that this was utilizing a $50 stock cost. 5% of $50 is $2.50. In this way, your stop-misfortune number would be $47.50 (50 - 2.50). If the stock value slides to $47.50, you would execute your trade and leave your situation with benefit close by.

By no means whatsoever, is this a hard and quick guideline because there are times when a more tightly stop-misfortune is suitable. Your options trading framework should reveal to you what is and what isn't proper for every specific trade. That is the reason you have your structure set up.

Keep in mind, and you are managing options. At the point when the market betrays your position, the majority of your benefits in addition to a few or the majority of your capital can vanish rapidly. You need to act quickly and not be reluctant to pull the trigger.

You never become penniless profiting. You need to benefit with options trading procedures. That is the reason you execute them in any case. Focus on your strategy, watch the market, and make a move. This should profit over the long haul.

Chapter 22: Do's and Don'ts

Finally, while all the information in this book should prepare you to enter the world of options trading with some degree of confidence, nothing can really prepare you for live trading. Every situation will be different and may require any one of the strategies we have discussed in this book or some combination of them. Although no one can possibly prepare any options trader for every conceivable transaction, event, or opportunity. Success in this field will come with continued application of the methods, strategies, and knowledge you have gained from this book, and that you will continue to learn as you successfully complete transactions with other investors. However, regardless of the specifics of any given options trade, there are some general "rules of the road" that most traders play by. This chapter includes what we consider to be the most important do's and don'ts of options trading. As you begin your career in this exciting field, we hope not only that you put these strategies work for you but also that you begin formulating your own compilation of road-tested options trading secrets.

Understand Market Basics

In the modern world, investment has been made accessible to the average person. Most employers who offer retirement savings plans often sponsor an education day, so employees can gain some familiarity with the types of retirement plans and options that are available to them. In addition, with the proliferation of cable news networks, specialized programming, the internet, and social media, there is no shortage of information widely available to virtually anyone, anywhere.

Especially in the information age, knowledge is power. Before you jump right into trading on the options market, take some time to familiarize yourself with the basics of market dynamics. Options traders use a language that is unique to their niche in the investment world, and many outsiders may be completely perplexed and unable to understand much of what they say. In addition, the ability to tolerate a certain amount of financial risk is an inseparable component of successful investing. Thus, by understanding not only the terminology of the options market but also the fundamental dynamics of the stock market in general, investors can exponentially increase their chances of assembling a profitable career in options trading.

Play by the Rules

As an options trader, you will be in competition with other traders and investors. Much of your success in investing--including making valuable connections in the investment world--will result from your ability to play by the rules. The stock market is a living thing, and the activity of traders has a huge impact on its health and volatility. We are all tempted to be maverick investors who leave a legacy of innovation, but understanding the fundamentals will work in your favor.

Specifically, option prices increase or decrease as a result of changes in share prices and volatility.

So, when share prices increase, call options make money and put options lose money; when share prices decrease, put options make money and call options lose money. Options also move in relation to volatility; when share prices are stable, greater volatility can increase the options pricing. So, when volatility increases, buying options makes money; when volatility decreases, selling options makes money.

Understanding these four basic rules can help you become a better trader.

Adapt Your Strategy to Market Conditions

Once you're up and running in the world of professional options trading, you will gain confidence as you see your efforts pay off in returns to your options account. As you move from a Level 1 trading account to a Level 2 trading account, you will likely develop a preference for a certain type of options trades—maybe covered calls or married puts. Familiarity with the language and mechanics of the options trading profession is definitely something that will work in your favor. However, it is important to remember that as you move up the ladder, you will gain access to a wider array of trading tools and strategies. As you gain knowledge and experience, remember that no matter how comfortable you have become with a select number of options trading strategies, there will always be additional aspects of nuance that can enhance your skill as a trader and increase the profitability of your efforts. The key to ensuring success is not just in choosing the best strategy in relation to the performance of the underlying asset. You must also consider the overall market conditions and whether those conditions may have an effect on the future performance of that asset. Although one strategy may have worked in the past under similar conditions, considering changes in current conditions will help you adjust your strategy to ensure you continue to build on your past success.

Always Have an Exit Plan

Picking a stock, formulating an options strategy to generate income from the stock's performance, and then contacting your broker to initiate an opening transaction is a good beginning. But this plan is not a complete strategy. The most important part of any options strategy is not how to get in—it's how to get out.

The payoff of an options strategy may result from buying the underlying stock at below market value, from accepting a cash settlement deposit for a put option on stock with declining value, or even from profiting from an increase in the cost of the options premium by selling the contract before it expires.

However, you believe the asset you have identified may provide you with an opportunity to construct a profitable options trading strategy, conjecture and hope should not be part of that strategy. Before you complete an opening transaction, make sure you are very clear about your specific goal for entering the contract. After you complete the opening transaction, you will be faced with one of three possible outcomes:

1. The market and the target stocks moved in the direction you predicted.

2. The market or the target stocks move in a direction you did not predict, resulting in unexpected losses.

3. The market or the target stocks move in a direction you did not predict, resulting in unexpected gains.

Similarly, you should have three responses ready for each of these developments:

1. If you are faced with the first result, you should have an exit strategy already prepared. Whatever else is happening around you, as long as your assets are on the right track, do not deviate from your plan.

2. If there are unexpected changes that are not favorable to your position on the underlying asset, what plan did you formulate to exit the contract so you can minimize your losses?

3. If there are unexpected changes that are favorable to your position on the underlying asset, what plan did you formulate to exit the contract so you can capitalize on these gains?

No matter what happens, make sure you can answer all 3 questions before you enter an options contract. Then, once you have laid the groundwork for a successful options trade, stick with your plan, even if you think you could make a few more dollars by improvising.

Doubling up to Cover Losses

"Doubling up" is a prime example of how an options trader may ignore his original exit strategy if the market or the underlying stocks fail to perform the way he had expected when he originally constructed his strategy.

For example, let's say a trader buys a call option for 100 shares of Company B, with a strike price of $45. At the time he purchased the call option, Company B was trading at $44. The trader expects the share price to rise to $47 before the contract expires. Immediately after the opening transaction, though, the stock price slips to $43.

The premium for a call option with a strike price of $45 is further out-of-the-money now than at opening, In addition, there's still plenty of time before expiration. As a result, to compensate for any potential losses if the stock rises to only $46, the trader may be tempted to "double up" by buying another $45 call option at the reduced premium price.

If this trader were only purchasing stocks, he may have celebrated the unexpected drop in share value and immediately purchased as many additional shares as possible, with a goal of greater long-term return. But options trading works differently. The options trader is focused on short-term returns, and if the stock price fails to put the contract in-the-money by the expiration date, the trader loses on not only one contract, but two.

The smart trader will remember that he created an exit plan for this scenario and will stick with it. Though it may be tempting to purchase an additional call option, he should judge the wisdom of such a purchase by asking himself if he would buy the second call option if he were not already in the middle of a trade. If this is not ordinarily a contract he would enter into--and it isn't, because that was definitely not his strategy in his opening transaction-- then market conditions and stock performance that defy expectations are probably the worst reasons for him to change that view.

Instead, he should either stay in his contract to see if the stock eventually rebounds and makes the contract profitable, or sell the contract immediately, cut his losses, and look for another opportunity that makes more sense.

Trying to Hit a "Home Run" Every Time

Popular culture portrays Wall Street as a sort of heaven for adrenaline junkies, in which highly skilled traders spend their days chasing down successively bigger, sexier, and more lucrative deals. The only barriers for these imaginary gods of the stock market appear to be failing to out-trade and outperform all their friends and colleagues and thereby missing out on bragging rights at the local pub at the end of the trading day.

A skilled options trader can make huge gains using well-planned strategies. Certainly, this should be a goal for every options trader, but it is a difficult goal to achieve for many reasons. First, the perfect storm of daily skyrocketing corporate share prices hardly ever occurs. Most stocks maintain stability and change very little from day to day, so the textbook conditions for a highly profitable options contract are hard to come by. As a result, if your approach to options trading strategies consists of trying to arrange contracts that guarantee payouts that are not likely to occur, or to approach market analysis from a perspective that a lesser degree of volatility is the exception rather than the rule, you will be missing the considerable opportunities the options trading market presents for disciplined investors.

Markets and indexes may not make dramatic swings very often, and that's probably a good thing. However, markets do consistently move by several points in both directions each day. By studying market behavior, you will have a better grasp of what types of changes are likely to occur and when. Using this knowledge to buy and sell options contracts that conform to sound market fundamentals can help you earn steady weekly returns. Practiced correctly, a well-disciplined approach to options trading can provide any skilled investor with the opportunity to create a source of steady residual income to enhance an existing portfolio.

Chapter 23: Buying and Selling Puts

Let's talk about buying and selling puts. Puts, of course, allow you to sell the stock that you have or the underlying commodity that you have underneath it all. There are different reasons why people may want to buy or sell puts, and here we'll go over what it is, how to do it, and the advantages of such.

What is Buying and Selling Puts?

Selling/buying puts essentially is giving someone the option to buy the stock at a certain amount of money.

If you sell a put option, you're selling the chance for someone to buy that stock at a price.

If you buy a put option, you're giving someone the option to buy that stock for that price and the person is obligated to sell it.

So, let's say that you're planning on getting a put option to buy that stock at a certain amount of money. You can put that option down, and from there, wait for it to fall, and from there you can exercise it. Maybe you want to buy shares from a really good railroad company. You essentially notice it's increasing the earnings on this, and you decide to buy the stock when it's under 30 potentially. By buying a put option, it basically makes the seller obligated to sell you the stock when it falls below 30 dollars.

You want to exercise these in falling markets since you'll generate a profit when the market is falling, rather than rising.

Selling Puts in this Market

Here's the thing, when you want to sell puts, you should only do so if you're comfy with the owning stock that's under it at the price that's there because essentially, you're assuming the obligation to buy it if the person does decide to sell. From this, you should also only enter trades where the net price paid for the security is good. This is the most important part of selling puts profitably in the markets that you have. There are other reasons to sell it to the person. You also can own the security below the market price that is currently there, and you'll definitely want to be careful when you do choose to sell this.

An Example of Buying a Put

Let us now move onto buying these puts. One thing to note is that you're not going to see the commissions, taxes, margins, and other charges factored into any of these equations for a reason. That starts to get it a bit more complicated, and right now, we are just showing you the cut and dry of all of the ways you can buy a put option that can be considered. But you should definitely consult with your tax advisor or broker before you go in.

So, the simplest way to bet against stocks is to get put options. Put options essentially give you that right to sell it at a certain price by a time period. You essentially pay the premium, which will from there will sell you that stock at that price.

So let's say you've got company A, which is overvalued currently at $50 bucks a share, and you decide to bet on a decline at this point, getting a put contract that's at $35 a share, and it costs $2 per share, so the "breakeven" price is $33 a share. This is deduced from basic math, since you're taking the contract price of 35 minus the 2 making it $33 for this. Since each of these represents 100 different shares. That's $3500 in total of what you'll buy, and then of course it'll cost you upfront $200 for this (cause of the options contract and the shares) and from there, you enter the trade.

Now, let's say that the option contract is for August 2019, and from there, you fast-forward and watch the market. Below is a table of what can happen

Action of stock What happens to you Your return Outlook

Soars all the way up to $60 The option expires, becomes worthless, and you lose the $200 premium, but you're basically losing nothing else (100%)

  Okay

Falls slightly to $38 Same thing happens, stock falls but you don't make a profit (100%)

  Okay

Drops all the way to $25 You make some cash! 800 dollars to be exact ($35-25) and then the $2 premium (800%) Nice!

Drops to $0 (basically going bankrupt) The ideal situation, and you'll get $3300 from it (0 at expiration, so 3500-200 from the premium) (1500%) Ideal!

So, the best time to use these is when you have a sinking ship in terms of stock. Otherwise, they aren't worth your time, and it's better not to have these stocks, and there is always a chance you could end up losing money. But, if the person sells the stock, and you turn around and cash in on it, you'll have more money, and you don't have to worry about the burden of a stock.

If you choose to buy it when it declines, you're essentially going to get money from this. You want to do it when it's declining and nothing more. It is very important that you don't choose to act on these types of options until it's that time.

That's it, that's all buying put options is, and you want to make sure that it falls to the level that you want it to be at.

The risks of it

Risks are still there in both cases. Options are risky due to the complex nature of this, but once you know how these works, it can reduce the risk a whole lot. Put options, in particular, can be quite risky, especially for the seller, since they may have to spend more money buying back the option that they once had.

One other aspect of this, especially for buyers is the break-even aspects of it. So, let's assume that you got a stock today for $46 and this was at $44, which is two points down what it is there, so you'll be profitable in the trade. But, here's the thing, you're going end up losing out on money due to the fee for the option. It would make the option worth $2 since you spent $4 on it, so that means you're losing out on it.

But there is also the fact that if the option does expire and you're in-the-money, you'll get the right stock immediately. You may not realize it, but these can be quite good, especially for plunging markets, especially if you know they will bounce back.

If you end up seeing it go high, you're going to end up paying for that premium to get the right to buy it, and that's money that can rack up to a couple of thousand dollars. Do make sure that you understand that when you do choose to figure out your own stock, and how you can easily rectify.

The Advantages of Buying Puts

Buying puts, which gives you an option to sell the stock at a given price, is good if you're looking to protect yourself. So, let's say that you have this stock, or you've been eyeing a stock that will probably fall, and then rise over the succeeding few months. There are those out there, and usually, it's due to lulls in the market at the time. So, you decide to buy the put that's there, which gives you the option to sell that stock when the market decides to resurface at a higher level.

For you, you're taking a gamble on this, because the market may not recover, but if you notice a stock that could potentially have the power to fall possibly, this may be a good one.

That way, you can get the stock for cheaper. From there, you can sell the stock again, and you have the right to sell that stock at the price that you're looking for.

It essentially allows you to form that extra security in his, which is a nice little advantage for the person who wants to sell it. Long puts are good for this, especially if you want to sell these.

Put options let you sell this asset at the strike price that's there. With this, the seller is then obligated to purchase these shares from the holder. Now, how can this help? Let's say that you buy a stock at 20 bucks, and then you compare it to 20 dollars at the edge that's there. If the price is below 20 at any point, you can actually then exercise the options and reduce the losses. This can definitely help, especially if you're willing to buy an option, and from there, sell it in order to avoid lots of trouble.

Naked Puts

There are also naked puts, which is an advanced put options strategy, so I don't suggest trying this till you've worked with basic puts. The reason for that is because of their incredibly risky.

What does it mean to trade an option naked though? It doesn't mean that you're going to the stock exchange in the buff, but rather, you're selling the options without having a position in the underlying instrument. For example, if you're writing a naked put, you're selling a put without having the stock.

The covered call is probably the most basic stock trading strategy. This strategy provides an ideal entry point for those who are new to options trading and allows them to turn their existing investment activities into a gateway for trading options. The premise of the covered call is quite simple. The idea behind this strategy is to minimize your cost basis on your stock purchases.

Let's take a look at how this works.

The best way to think about a covered call is to look at it as a method to earn dividends on your stock holdings. While a stock may or may not pay you a dividend, with a covered call strategy you can earn income on the position and therefore lower your effective purchase price. Another way of looking at this is to view it as turning your stock purchase into a bond which pays you monthly or bi-monthly interest.

So how does it work? Well, the strategy has two legs to it.

1. A long stock

2. A short call

Execution

The long stock leg is simply your investment purchase in a stock. A lot of people who get into trading already hold shares as part of a retirement account or some other portfolio. If you already hold a position in some stock, then employing this strategy will work wonders for you.

The execution is pretty straightforward. You already hold long stock or establish a long stock position in some company that you think has good long-term prospects. I must emphasize that this leg is all about investment and it has nothing to do with speculation. Whatever research you do to purchase this stock should be done on the basis of sound investment principles. So, you need to be aware of the earning ability of the company and its long-term prospects. Do not purchase stock just to execute a covered call.

Chapter 24: The Most Common Questions about Trading

1. Can you live on trading?

Yes, just as you can live from medicine, from being a teacher, from being an architect, engineer, or lawyer. You require the same weapons: education, training, practice, guidance, discipline, perseverance, and a lot of determination to be a great professional in your field. Trading is no different. Perhaps many people have been wrong to think that when opening an account in a broker, funding their accounts, and starting trading means having the results to live from trading in less than what a rooster sings and being millionaires. Very wrong!!! It's like pretending to be a surgeon overnight. If you can live from trading, the question is, do you have what it takes to do it and achieve it?

2. What do I do to start trading?

The first and most important thing is to educate yourself about what trading is and how to do it effectively. Start by knowing the nature of trading, what it is about, how you win, who participates, how is the market that has been chosen, etc., are some of the things you should keep in mind. Don't get to war empty-handed. Go prepared. How? Find someone to inspire you, to teach these things, to guide you, invest money and time in your education. There are many online trading schools, and you can be overwhelmed at first by searching, but choose the one that has a simple system, that its philosophy resonates with you, and that has your feet set on the ground. Avoid those that promote phrases like "fast millionaire trading in the Stock Exchange," "trading is straightforward," etc. You have to be realistic, and a school that tells you from the beginning what is trading, how it works, how it is earned, how it is lost and that it is not as easy as many want to make it believe in profiting, is a school that is worth considering.

3. When will I start seeing results?

When you have firmly rooted in a simple trading system, faithfully and disciplined, fulfilling your trading plan and adequately managing the risk-benefit, paradoxically, you will also begin to see the results when you detach yourself from the results and focus on the process. The process of trading involves the observation and reflection of our performance, the emotions experienced, the most frequent mistakes and annihilation, the analysis of the logbook, and the correction of the things that you can change and improve. You will begin to see results when, in addition to all these things, you continue working on your mind without giving up.

4. How much money can I start trading, and what broker should I use?

It depends on each broker and the instrument you use. If you want to trade stock options in Thinkorswim, for example, you will need at least $ 2,000 to access the options. If you're going to trade with stocks, you will need $ 25,000. With the other brokers, it will be different. On the website of the brokers are the most frequent questions and customer service that can take you from all doubts regarding minimum money to start, documents such as funds and how to remove, etc. Find the broker that is regulated, that has a good reputation, that other people are using and tell you about their experience.

5. How much money per month can I generate by trading?

The one that allows you the size of your account and the amount you are going to invest per operation, as long as you have the capabilities required to make money consistently. This brings us to question # 1. It's that easy.

6. How to achieve consistency?

Consistency is achieved by having consistent behaviors and actions. That is, if I have planned trading that tells me what it looks like an opportunity, where to go, where to place the stop, how to manage and how to manage risk, and do it over and over again which tells me that plan consistently then I'll have consistent results. But if you change the policy, each has a stop or every time you have a losing streak then you will go into an endless loop in which as emotional and impatient trader will modify or change it again and again, the plan and the results will be different. This is what happens to 95% who lose money doing trading; there is no clear, defined, and precise plan to follow consistently, disciplined, and with a lot of confidence.

7. What is the best strategy or trading system?

The one that is simple to understand, that you can even explain it to a child and the child understands it. Stay away from those systems that require more than five different indicators, that your attention away from price action scribbles filling your screen and does not have proper management of risk-benefit. The best strategy or system is simple, clear, proven (functional), and above all, fits your personality and type of trader. The method of a trader may not be the system that suits you; for that reason, you must define what type of trader you are if you are scalper, intraday or swing, and of course, your risk tolerance (conservative or risky). These are just a few things to consider when choosing a trading system.

8. I have lost much of my capital; what do I do?

If you have lost a large part of your capital, it is because you do not have a clear, defined and proven trading plan, there are no consistent behaviors that lead to consistent results; emotions dominate you, and there is also no proper risk-benefit management. In that sentence is the answer to this question. What you should do is simple: make a clear trading plan with a clear and straightforward strategy, try it in a demo, manage risk-benefit properly, trust 100% in your plan, work on your emotions being aware of them before, during and after of operations, record, and evaluate to be able to learn from your failures.

If the results are positive, return to real account and repeat the process focusing your attention on the emotions you experience and your reactions.

9. What actions do you recommend operating to start?

I recommend trading stocks that do not have a widespread, that are not very volatile and offer economic contracts near ITM. These are terms that you may not understand if you are starting. Once you know what the ideal requirements are, go to the Finviz map of actions and look for the best-known actions in each sector, write them down, go to your platform and look at their contract and spread grid, so you are choosing and removing from the list until have your ideal portfolio of at least 6 shares.

10. I have no time to trading regularly, what are my options?

You can choose to do swing trading. The swing will allow you to open an operation today and close it several days later. You will need a trading system that suits this style, have your stop defined so that it protects your capital while you are away, and periodically review operations. Some brokers have mobile applications that allow you to monitor operations from your cell phone. If the situation is that you cannot trade in the morning, you can choose to make a trading plan for the afternoon hours, and it will work the same.

Conclusion

An option trading is a daunting concept for those who never did. They've probably heard tales from people who claim to have made incredible profits or from someone who says, "I've lost too much money too quickly." I hope this GUIDE can help you understand how both of those things might happen, and what one you might have is up to.

While options are financial securities, like futures and swaps, and they have a fungible value that is exchanged on exchanges just like anyone else, they behave differently. It is therefore important that you understand their nature fully before putting any money in the line.

Two types of options are available: puts and calls. Anyone who owns a put has the right – but not the duty – to sell the put security at a certain price before the put expires. Those who own a call have the right-but not the duty-to buy their basic security (at a price, before expiry).

The language of the 'right, but not the duty' is why such instruments are after all called choices and why they can be so attractive. Option owners only eventually take a short or long role in the underlying market if the market shifts in a lucrative direction.

However, both a buyer and a seller are traded in each contract. An individual who buys a place is boring for the underlying market of security and would be profitable if the price goes below its strike price, but no additional duty if the price is higher.

On the other hand, anyone who sold this item is bullish for the underlying protection. He hopes the stock will never slip below the strike price until expiry, and the put will never be exercised. When the putting is done, the seller is on the hook to buy the underlying security from the put owner at the price.

If the underlying market has fallen significantly below the strike price, the seller may have seen very serious, very brisk declines in his portfolio and since the options market is traded much more thinly than the shares, a seller will often find it hard to break out of that obligation.

The same applies to call vendors-if the demand goes above the call strike price, the call owner may want to exercise the right and purchase protection at the strike price. The seller of the call will sell it to him at the strike price. Then, when the short investor reaches the higher market price of the underlying security, he is hit with a loss.

Such losses to the seller can only occur if options are "in the bank." You may have learned these words from individuals who have been using options in trade before. One alternative could be one of three: out - of-the-money: a put is out - of-money if the security is currently higher than the put-in price.

A call is out - of-money if the security underlying the call is lower than the price of the call. So, any out of the money option gives its owner no inherent advantage. If the underlying security is actually priced at the same price of the attack, options are considered cash. However, you can imagine how low the odds are and how rarely opportunities for money are exercised.

In - the-money: A put is in - the-money if the security is currently less than the put strike price. A call is in the money if the security underlying the call is greater than the cost of the attack. T

that is when the right is offered by the investor, since the underlying protection is profitably bought and sold at such price disparities. Also, when the seller of the option is swallowing bullets, he's now on the hook for the loss.

And the only thing an option seller can do is that the right never moves in the money and is never exercised and it ends worthlessly.

He sold it at a certain premium value (the buyer is expected to pay the seller the amount, like a premium on an investment, for the ability to make an offer while the market is moving somewhat), even if it is worthless, he will never have to buy it back or have the underlying coverage and will maintain the full premium he got at the time he sold it.

The seller can also opt out by buying it back and either benefit or lose on the increase in the premium value before it expires. Options holders may also seek to obtain any of the premium charged by selling before the option expires.

But if the buyer or seller wants to get out of the trade, they must do it before Friday expires. Options whose underlying security is stocks or indices, with quarterly expiry dates, are issued, such that all such calls will expire every three months, on the third Friday of a quarter of each month in the last month.

People with options trading also attempt to close their positions right before this occurs, which makes the markets particularly volatile on those days.

All who uses options trading has justification to do so. Optional sellers wish to receive premiums with the expectation that the demand does not surpass a pre-expiration level.

Thus, they can be bullish or bearish depending on whether they sell puts or calls. They may also have an idea of the market, and take advantage of their idea by selling telephone spreads.

In the meantime, option owners are not responsible for margin calls when the market moves in the opposite direction-either bullish or Bearish. You have to pay for this chance-often dearly. Another fascinating consumer of the options, however, is the heel: the one who uses other instruments and buys options now to defend himself against failure.

There is a fair chance of using options trading for both of these purposes but it is so important that you know what the other side of your trading is encouraging, and you know clearly what your risks are and your future advantages.

www.ingramcontent.com/pod-product-compliance
Lightning Source LLC
Chambersburg PA
CBHW080459220526
45465CB00006B/2318